AN APPROACH TO 'HAMLET'

AN APPROACH TO
'HAMLET'

L. C. KNIGHTS

Winterstoke Professor of English in the
University of Bristol

STANFORD UNIVERSITY PRESS
STANFORD, CALIFORNIA
1961

Library of Congress Catalog
Card Number: 61-6216

Stanford University Press
Stanford, California
© L. C. Knights 1960
PRINTED IN GREAT BRITAIN

For

BENJAMIN AND FRANCES

Contents

Author's Note

THESE lectures were prepared for the Birmingham Uni
versity Summer School of 1959 at Stratford-on-Avon.
Their reception there encouraged me to think that
they might be of some interest to a wider audience. I
have however kept the informal tone, and the lectures
are presented substantially as they were delivered. In
Lecture One I helped myself to a dozen sentences from
an end-note in *Some Shakespearean Themes*; since the
borrowed material cannot now be excised I apologize
to any reader who notices the repetition. Indeed the
present book, although it stands by itself, can be
regarded as in some ways a supplementary chapter to
the former one.

I owe an especial debt to my friend, H. D. F. Kitto,
Professor of Greek in the University of Bristol, for
allowing me to use for my own purposes what he has
written on *Hamlet*. I can only hope that he will not
think I have abused his kindness. Acknowledgements
are also made to Messrs. Methuen and Co. Ltd. for
permission to quote from Professor Kitto's book *Form
and Meaning in Drama*.

L. C. K.

Bristol University,

August, 1959

I

I

*H*AMLET is, I suppose, that play of Shakespeare's about which there is most disagreement. There is no need for me to remind you of the bewildering variety of different things that have been said both about the Prince of Denmark and his play; it is enough to remark that more has been written about *Hamlet* than about any other of Shakespeare's plays, and that if, in the twentieth century, *Hamlet* has yielded to *King Lear* the distinction of being the play in which the age most finds itself, there is still no lack of widely differing interpretations of the former piece. Indeed I once decided that if ever I should write or talk about *Hamlet* at any length—a task that I have shirked up to now—I should use as my title 'Through the Looking-Glass', so clear is it that, more than with any other play, critics are in danger of finding reflected what they bring with them to the task of interpretation, so difficult is it, once you are in the play, to be sure of the right direction. And it is not many months since a writer in the *Listener* remarked that 'every fresh critic who sets out to define the intentions of the author of *Hamlet* ends up in his own particular dead-end in queer street'. So the hazards are, it seems, considerable.

Let me, therefore, call attention to my title, which is not 'An Interpretation of *Hamlet*' but 'An Approach to *Hamlet*'. Interpretation is of course involved; but what I want to emphasize is, first, that the interpretation is tentative—a kind of thinking aloud which I hope will be found useful by other people; and, secondly, that I propose to set the play in relation to other plays of Shakespeare, to try to see it in a particular perspective, rather than to attempt a detailed commentary.

Hamlet belongs to the year 1600 or to the early months of 1601. It thus comes near the beginning of a period when Shakespeare was much concerned with the relationship between the mind, the whole reflective personality, and the world with which it engages. Particularly he seems to have been preoccupied with distortions in men's way of looking at the world; and the plays in which this preoccupation is active raise, in various ways, the problem of the relation of 'knowledge' to the knower, to what a man is, to the true or distorted imagination. What I wish to do in this first lecture is to bring some of these plays together, not in strict chronological order, nor indeed in any strictly systematic way, but simply to elicit what—for all their difference—they have in common, and to see if their linked preoccupations may not form a context for the play towards which, in the remaining three lectures, our attention will be mainly directed.

There is no need for me to tell you that Shakespeare, from time to time, showed a very considerable preoccupation with man's subjection to illusion, 'the seeming truth which cunning times put on To entrap the wisest' (*M. of V.* III. ii. 100-101); it was a preoccupation that noticeably deepened in the period immediately preceding the great tragedies. Now the question posed by the undoubted power of illusion branches in two directions, towards the deceiver, and towards the deceived. Shakespeare, like many another writer, was certainly interested in the deceiver, especially the one who does not merely assume a deliberate disguise, like Iago, but is false in subtler ways, like Cressida, or deceives himself as well as others, like Angelo—of whom the Duke said, 'Hence shall we see, If power change purpose, what our seemers be'. But his main interest seems to have centred on the deceived, and a question that he asks with some insistence is how men come to make false or distorted judgments about other persons or about the world at large—what it is in their own natures that makes them capable of being deceived. This preoccupation seems to be present in two of the middle comedies. At all events, in *Much Ado about Nothing* (1598) the credence given to the slanderer may well be intended, as Mr. James Smith has suggested, to precipitate a judgment on the society represented by Claudio and Don Pedro (*Scrutiny*, XIII, 4, 1946). And I would tentatively suggest that *All's Well that Ends Well*—that unsatisfactory play (1602-3)—only makes sense when it is seen as a kind of morality play in which Bertram is for long unable to recognize his true good in Helena.

II

Both *Troilus and Cressida* (c. 1602) and *Othello* (1603) pursue the problem at a much deeper level. *Troilus and Cressida* is far too complex a play to be dealt with briefly, and here a few words must suffice. I have tried to show elsewhere[1] how both Greeks and Trojans are presented as subjected to time and appearance—the Greeks, because they stand for public life and an impersonal 'reason', divorced from feeling and intuitive intelligence; the Trojans, their complementary opposites, because their way of life is based on a passionate and wilful assertion of the untutored self. The play, as I said, is complex. For our present purposes it is enough to note how Shakespeare presents Troilus, not simply as the victim of Cressida's unfaithfulness but as, to some extent, self-deceived. The way in which he meets experience is both presented and, I think, criticized in the poetry that is given him to speak—the poetry through which his attitude to life is defined. Of this, Mr D. A. Traversi, in an essay published twenty years ago (*Scrutiny*, VII, 3, 1938) gave a classic account. In the imagery of the love poetry, there is, he says, 'a poignant thinness', which conveys simultaneously 'an impression of intense feeling and an underlying lack of content'. Of a characteristic passage he remarked: 'The emotions are intense enough, but only in the palate and the senses; they scarcely involve any full personality in the speaker'. And Traversi further pointed out that the expression of Troilus's 'idealism' through the imagery of taste underlines its unsubstantiality and its subjection to time. It is, we may say, the over-active element of subjective fantasy in Troilus's passion that gives to his love poetry its hurried, fevered note, with a suggestion of trying to realize something essentially unrealizable; it is his intense subjectivism that commits him to a world of time and appearance. At the risk of

[1] In *Some Shakespearean Themes*, Chapter IV.

drawing an over-simple moral from a complicated play,
I would put the matter thus: if both Troilus and the
Greeks are shown as 'fools of time', this is not because
there is something hostile to men's hopes and aspira-
tions in the very nature of things, so that 'checks and
disasters' necessarily 'grow in the veins of actions
highest reared'; it is because of some failure at deep
levels of the personality, which can be called indiffer-
ently a failure of reason or of the imagination. If this is
right it marks an interesting connexion with *Othello*,
where attention centres on those elements in Othello's
mind and feelings, his attitudes towards himself, that
make him so vulnerable to Iago.

III

On *Othello* there are two brilliant essays—one by
Wilson Knight, in *The Wheel of Fire*, and one by F. R.
Leavis, in *The Common Pursuit*; to both of them I am
very much indebted, and I wish to mention them
before going on to suggest how the play develops the
theme—the relationship between self and world—that
is our present concern.

Othello, we may say, defines the peculiar weakness
and vulnerability—the capacity for being deceived—
of a particular attitude to life. That attitude is defined
and made present to our imaginations through a mode
of speech. Othello's character is given us not only by
what he says but by the way he says it, within the
accepted conventions of poetic drama,[1] and I must ask

[1] This is an obvious instance of what Mr Arthur Sewell, in his
most helpful book, *Character and Society in Shakespeare*, calls 'the
distillation of personality into style'.

you to call that style to mind before I go on to make the observation that will link this play with those others with which I wish to associate it. Almost any of Othello's utterances when he is truly himself will serve. Take for example his reply to Iago's excited account of how Brabantio is incensed against him:

> Let him do his spite:
> My services, which I have done the signiory,
> Shall out-tongue his complaints. 'Tis yet to know—
> Which, when I know that boasting is an honour,
> I shall promulgate—I fetch my life and being
> From men of royal siege, and my demerits
> May speak unbonneted to as proud a fortune
> As this that I have reached.

Consciousness of worth is expressed in every line, not only in explicit statement but in tone and movement; and the lofty tone is emphasized by phrases that are the opposite of common or idiomatic. A moment later we have,

> But that I love the gentle Desdemona,
> I would not my unhoused free condition
> Put into circumscription and confine
> For the sea's worth . . .

—where there is suggested for the first time Othello's nostalgic feeling for the life of action, 'the pride, pomp, and circumstance of glorious war'. Our impression is made up of a sense of calm and assured dignity, of something a little exotic, and of Othello's consciousness of worth—'My parts, my title and my perfect [fully prepared] soul'.

This is the Othello whom we see in the next scene, when, with grave deliberation, he makes his defence against Brabantio before the Venetian Senate:

Most potent, grave, and reverend signiors,
My very noble and approved good masters. . . .

How different this is, in tone and manner, from the quick, nervous phrasing of Macbeth! Of course Othello goes on to tell us something about himself which would be important however he told it: he has been a soldier all his life,

And little of this great world can I speak,
More than pertains to feats of broil and battle . . .

but the manner is equally important. 'Pertains' brings out the unidiomatic quality; the phrasing is 'monumental'. At the same time there is a suggestion of poetry in the way Othello sees himself:

For since these arms of mine had seven years pith,
Till now some nine moons wasted, they have used
Their dearest action in the tented field.

A romantic glamour is thrown over the kind of life Othello has lived, and over himself as someone eminently suited to lead that kind of life. The romantic note is developed when he goes on to tell of his wooing:

Wherein I spake of most disastrous chances,
Of moving accidents by flood and field,
Of hair-breadth scapes i' the imminent deadly breach,
Of being taken by the insolent foe,
And sold to slavery, of my redemption thence,
And portance in my travel's history . . .

'Imminent', 'redemption', 'portance'—all have a latin-
ized or foreign flavour, just as the Cannibals—the
Anthropophagi—who come in a moment later, are
obviously exotic. And with this goes an unconscious
egotism:

> She loved me for the dangers I had pass'd,
> And I loved her that she did pity them.

It is also important to realize that what Wilson Knight
calls 'the Othello music', the Othello idiom, is one that
does not engage very closely with actuality. Value is
insistently attributed to what is remote, or to that
world of simplified action where Othello was, so to
speak, at home—the world so far removed from that
Cyprus where he is called on to meet the new
experience of getting to know the wife who loved
him.

Now it is precisely this Othello who succumbs—and
succumbs so promptly—to Iago in the temptation
scene. This is in essentials the point that Leavis makes
so well in the essay to which I have referred. The speed
with which Iago successfully develops his attack Leavis
explains in terms of something self-centred and self-
regarding in Othello's love—something that prevents
him from seeing Desdemona fully as a complete person.
What Iago can exploit is not only Othello's romantic
naïvety, his ignorance of all but the world of external
affairs, but Othello's consciousness of his own worth—
'I would not have your free and noble nature Out of
self bounty be abused'. On the tremendous and awful
vow that Othello makes when he finally commits
himself to revenge—

>   Like to the Pontic sea,
> Whose icy current and compulsive course
> Ne'er feels retiring ebb . . .
> Even so my bloody thoughts, with violent pace,
> Shall ne'er look back . . .

Leavis comments: 'At this climax of the play, as he sets himself irrevocably in his vindictive resolution, he reassumes formally his heroic self-dramatization—reassumes the Othello of "the big wars that make ambition virtue". The part of this conscious nobility, this noble egotism, this self-pride that was justified by experience irrelevant to the present trials and stresses, is thus underlined. Othello's self-idealization, his promptness to jealousy and his blindness are shown in their essential relation.'

It is for reasons such as these that Othello is vulnerable to Iago—that Iago who is so much less than a fully drawn 'character' whose motives we are invited to examine, and so much more than a mere 'necessary piece of dramatic mechanism'. What we have to notice here is that Iago's mode of speech is at the opposite pole from Othello's. It is idiomatic, whereas Othello's is rhetorical; it is realistic, drawing readily on the commonplace and everyday, whereas Othello's is exotic; and it conveys a persistent animus.[1] Iago's vocabulary, his idiom, imagery and allusions, come from a world in which the common is the commonplace: cumulatively, the suggestion is of a world not only without glamour but without ideals, the world of conventional jokes about women—'to make fools laugh i' the alehouse',

---

[1] Leavis speaks of Iago's 'deflating, unbeglamouring, brutally realistic mode of speech'.

as Desdemona says. There is of course nothing wrong with common idiom as such. The point is that Iago uses it to deflate: there is almost invariably animus either against the object to which he applies his comparisons, or against the subject from which his comparisons and references are drawn. Iago's world is one in which things and people are manipulated, a world completely without values; and his manner of speech gives expression to a view of life that attributes reality to nothing but the senses and the will: 'Virtue! a fig! 'tis in ourselves that we are thus or thus.' Taking notice of these things we may say with Wilson Knight that Iago is 'the spirit of denial, wholly negative', adding also that it is precisely this coarse, reductive cynicism against which an egocentric romanticism is so defenceless. Iago, as Maud Bodkin says, is 'the shadow-side of Othello'.[1] What the play gives in the temptation scene and later is something like possession —possession by foul imaginings. This too is reflected in Othello's language when it becomes as coarse and brutal as Iago's.

Let me now draw these reflections to a point where they may be seen to fit into the general argument. Grace Stuart, in her book *Narcissus: a Psychological Study of Self-Love*, speaks of Othello as a Narcissist who tries to make of the woman with whom he fell in love a mirror for his idealized self, or for those qualities in himself that he found most acceptable, and it is clear that it is, fundamentally, a failure to love that makes the tragedy. But besides this, the moral centre of the play, there is what may be called the metaphysical

[1] *Archetypal Patterns of Poetry*, Chapter V.

centre, and although the two are inseparable they may
be distinguished. At the height of his perplexity
Othello twice refers to Iago's ability to know:

> This honest creature doubtless
> Sees and knows more, much more, than he unfolds.

> This fellow's of exceeding honesty,
> And knows all qualities, with a learned spirit,
> Of human dealings . . .

The question at the heart of the play is, in the moral
world, the world of human relationships, what can we
know? The answer is, we know only what our habitual
categories and modes of thought—formed by our
whole disposition—allow us to know. Iago (witness his
idiom and habitual turn of phrase) lives in the world of
the knowing wink: his categories are reductive ('nothing but'). Now there are aspects of the world that these
categories, to some extent, fit: some women are as Iago
describes them, and Roderigo is a fool—though even
here his animus and perverse satisfaction in seeing the
worst severely limit his knowledge. Where the categories are worse than useless Iago can only know a
travesty: 'The Moor is of a free and open nature. . . .
And will as tenderly be led by the nose as asses are':
that is all Iago knows about an open nature. But
Othello's categories, also, are not framed to give him
true knowledge about human life. His romantic self-
dramatization leaves him at the mercy of the 'knowing'
man, or of that demon of cynicism that masks itself as
disillusioned knowledge. To know it is necessary to
love—to love with that outgoing generosity of spirit

for which this play constantly finds the word 'free'. Othello 'is of a free and open nature'; that is, he has the potentiality of freedom; but, as the play shows him, he is not fundamentally free, and the tragedy traces his deepening entanglement in illusion. What Othello represents—and this is where the play comes home to each one of us—is a particularly exalted conception of the self, a picture of 'me' as 'I' should like to appear— and as to some extent I may appear—but which, because it *is* a picture, is necessarily static, a fixed posture. This posture, moreover, is the opposite to a ready responsiveness to life as it comes to meet me: it is self-dramatizing and self-regarding, and to that extent it is a barrier against the knowledge that would bring freedom.

IV

We can now go on to a final consideration. In the plays we have just glanced at the wrong judgments are completely wrong. In *Julius Caesar* (1599), which came shortly before *Hamlet*, and in *Timon of Athens*, which I think (though there is much scholarly opinion against me) came shortly before *King Lear*, the interest shifts to the distorting intrusion of subjective elements, even when the facts of the case as presented are such as go a long way to justify Brutus's or Timon's view of the world.

Since time is not unlimited, and since I want to keep the main lines of my argument clear, I shall say little about *Julius Caesar*. There are, I think, three main points to be made. (i) The political situation—the situation created by Caesar's rise to power—is complex; and although there is clearly some truth in the unfavourable view of Caesar, the situation as a whole does not allow of a simple judgment. (ii) Brutus does so simplify: he concentrates on a selection of the facts before him in the interests of an abstract view of 'the general good':

> It must be by his death: and for my part,
> I know no personal cause to spurn at him,
> But for the general . . .

(iii) In this way Brutus does not only involve himself in a web of specious argument (as in the soliloquy from which I have just quoted), he constructs an unreal world: and because this world—the world where his decisions are formed—does not correspond with the real world—the world where acts have necessary consequences—his actions are disastrous. In other words, Brutus deceives himself because, like other characters in this play, he tries to make the public world, the political world, completely independent of the world of living men known in direct personal relationships. There is no time to develop this, but I think there is no doubt at all that the play consistently emphasizes both the 'public'/'private' contrast that I have just mentioned, and the lack of correspondence between Brutus's imaginings and the reality.

> O! that we then could come by Caesar's spirit,
> And not dismember Caesar. But, alas!
> Caesar must bleed for it. And, gentle friends,
> Let's kill him boldly, but not wrathfully;
> Let's carve him as a dish fit for the gods,
> Not hew him as a carcass fit for hounds.

That is not how political murders are carried out, as the play takes care to remind us later:

> . . . when your vile daggers
> Hack'd one another in the sides of Caesar:
> You show'd your teeth like apes, and fawn'd like hounds . . .
> Whilst damned Casca, like a cur behind,
> Struck Caesar on the neck.

The incongruity between intention and effect is ironically underlined in the excited proclamation after the murder—

> And, waving our red weapons o'er our heads,
> Let's all cry 'Peace, freedom, and liberty!'

—for the upshot of course is neither peace nor republican liberty, and the whole play may be taken as a comment on the words of Cicero,

> But men may construe things after their fashion,
> Clean from the purpose of the things themselves.

Julius Caesar, in short, is not a play where we are required to take sides for or against Caesar; it is a powerful study of one of the sources of illusion in public life; particularly it is a study of the distortion of a complex actuality by an abstracting, simplifying habit of mind, working in the interests, not of life, but of 'reasons of state'.[1]

V

Timon of Athens is a play of many problems, and the one towards which I want to direct your attention in

[1] I have developed this in 'Shakespeare's Political Wisdom', *Sewanee Review*, LXI, 1, Winter, 1953.

such time as remains is the largest of them, for it concerns the nature of Timon's misanthropy. Put simply, it is that the speeches of disgust and vituperation addressed to mankind at large are extraordinarily powerful, yet at the same time distorted and excessive, and the problem is to know how we are to take them. It does not seem to me adequate to regard them as expressing the disillusioned revulsion of a noble nature. Nor, with the superb artistic control of *King Lear* in mind, does it seem profitable to consider the view, once popular, that Shakespeare is here indulging a merely personal, unbalanced rage. When, betrayed by his false friends, Timon has turned his back on Athens, why does his denunciation take the particular form it does? More especially, why is his first long soliloquy, after the mock banquet, 'without the walls of Athens' (IV. i), so full of sexual nausea, for which nothing so far in the play has prepared us?

> Let me look back upon thee. O thou wall,
> That girdest in those wolves, dive in the earth,
> And fence not Athens! Matrons turn incontinent!
> Obedience fail in children! Slaves and fools,
> Pluck the grave wrinkled senate from the bench,
> And minister in their steads! To general filths
> Convert, o' the instant, green virginity!
> Do't in your parents' eyes! Bankrupts, hold fast;
> Rather than render back, out with your knives,
> And cut your trusters' throats! Bound servants, steal!
> Large-handed robbers your grave masters are,
> And pill by law. Maid, to thy master's bed!
> Thy mistress is o' the brothel. Son of sixteen,

Pluck the lined crutch from thy old limping sire,
With it beat out his brains! Piety, and fear,
Religion to the gods, peace, justice, truth,
Domestic awe, night-rest, and neighbourhood,
Instruction, manners, mysteries, and trades,
Degrees, observances, customs, and laws,
Decline to your confounding contraries,
And yet confusion live!

Now it is true that Timon has reason to be bitterly
disillusioned and angry; the Senate is usuring—so we
have been led to suppose—the Lords of Athens are
monsters of meanness, 'friendship' and 'society' have
been found false. But what are matrons, maids, and sons
doing here? and why are they exhorted to drown themselves in an anarchy compounded of incontinence and
impiety? It can of course be said that for Timon, as for
others, once 'the bonds of heaven' are 'loos'd' in any
particular instance there seems nothing to prevent a
general dissolution of all 'sanctimonies' (the concluding
lines of my quotation seem to justify this use of the
terminology of *Troilus and Cressida*). In fact, however,
the play has shown nothing to justify this wholesale
indictment, resting as it does on the assumption of
general evil, and making more of 'lust and liberty',
with their accompanying diseases, than of the betrayal
of friendship, which we have in fact observed.

For an explanation we have to wait until Timon's
next outburst in IV, iii.[1] This scene—'Enter Timon
from the cave'—opens with a superb indictment that,

[1] The intervening scene is given to the loyal Steward, Flavius, and
the servants, and its general effect is to restore Timon to a more
favourable light ('so noble a master,' 'kind lord'), whilst still leaving
us with a question about his 'goodness' and 'bounty'.

unlike the previous soliloquy, has the whole force of the play, of what has been demonstrated in the play, behind it, the first seventeen lines being concerned almost exclusively with the difference that mere material goods can make to a man's standing.

> Who dares, who dares,
> In purity of manhood stand upright,
> And say, 'This man's a flatterer'? if one be,
> So are they all; for every grise of fortune
> Is smooth'd by that below: the learned pate
> Ducks to the golden fool . . .

Then, before the theme of money's power is taken up again, comes once more the comprehensive misanthropy:

> all is oblique;
> There's nothing level in our cursed natures
> But direct villany. Therefore, be abhorr'd
> All feasts, societies, and throngs of men!
> His semblable, yea, himself, Timon disdains:
> Destruction fang mankind!

'His semblable, yea, himself, Timon disdains.' This, it seems to me, forms the climax of the play, casting a retrospective light over the opening scenes, where Timon was shown at the height of his fortunes. If there had been any doubt of how we should take them (and there shouldn't, really, have been any), none remains. The purpose of Timon's so much emphasized 'bounty' was to buy a flattering picture of himself. 'You see, my lord, how ample you're beloved'—remarks such as this are the 'sacrificial whisperings' rained in his ear. And the stage directions confirm the impression of an inordinate thirst for approval: Timon's first approach is heralded with 'trumpets'; at the 'great banquet' with 'loud music' of the play's second scene, 'they all stand ceremoniously looking on Timon'[1]; and during the masque, 'the Lords rise from table, with much adoring of Timon'. There is indeed, as Apemantus remarks, much 'serving of becks and jutting-out of bums'. And it is not only Apemantus, the professional cynic, who reveals these feasts as 'pomps and vain-glories', nor a mere Senator who sees them as 'raging waste'. To the trustworthy Flavius it is a 'flow of riot',

> When all our offices have been oppress'd
> With riotous feeders, when our vaults have wept
> With drunken spilth of wine, when every room
> Hath blaz'd with lights and bray'd with minstrelsy.

When, again in Flavius' words, 'the means are gone that buy this praise', the flattering picture—like the one the painter brought for sale—is gone too. Morally, as well as materially, there is nothing that Timon can take from Athens,

> —Nothing I'll bear from thee
> But nakedness, thou detestable town!

—indeed a datum of the play is that *this* society has nothing to offer.[2] It is as completely unaccommodated man that Timon is forced to look within, and, finding himself hateful ('yea, himself, Timon disdains'), what he finds within he projects onto the world at large.

---

[1] This stage direction was, I find, added by Johnson; but the action seems to be indicated by the text.

[2] See J. C. Maxwell's Introduction to the New Cambridge edition of the play.

Hence the sweeping and inclusive disgust of the first soliloquy outside the walls of Athens. The attempt to buy assurance has failed, and the instinctive movement is flight, from the self as much as from society, leading inevitably to death. Apemantus, for all his exaggerated cynicism, is allowed to say some true things, and we feel that in his exchanges with Timon in IV, iii he makes a 'placing' comment: 'The middle of humanity thou never knewest, but the extremity of both ends. . . . An thou hadst hated meddlers sooner, thou should'st have loved thyself better now'. Timon has taken on the Apemantus role—indeed, as has been said, 'Apemantus is what Timon becomes'[1]—and the first thing we are told about Apemantus is that he is one 'that few things loves better Than to abhor himself'.

The question that we find ourselves pondering, therefore, as we read this play, is—In what ways is a statement, true in itself, like Timon's account of his false friends, vitiated by a failure of integrity in the person making it? In other words, the question concerning the validity of Timon's judgment of society is subordinate to the question—How did Timon come to feel like this? How does a man reach such extremes of hatred and rejection? And the conclusion to which the play leads us is that although Timon, in his denunciation of Athens, of mankind, may say some true

---

[1] 'Apemantus is what Timon becomes. . . . Even in the first three acts, though Apemantus and Timon are opposites, they are oddly drawn towards each other, as if they found a peculiar importance in each other's company. . . . They are, as it were, two aspects of a single self, the extremes between which the personality of a human being can alternate.' Geoffrey Bush, *Shakespeare and the Natural Condition*, p. 62.

things, he speaks from an attitude that is itself flawed. Since the purpose of his bounty seems to have been, at least in part, to purchase a flattering picture of himself, the misanthropy that results when the picture is destroyed is in effect a violent expression of self-dislike; and this is true even though the world of the play presents plenty of matter for denunciation.[1]

Similar considerations are, I believe, relevant to *Hamlet*. For the world with which Hamlet has to deal is indeed evil, and the play shows convincingly what may be called the logic of corruption; but the emotions and attitudes that Hamlet brings to bear when he confronts that world are themselves the subject of a radical questioning.

[1] After completing this section I found some support for my view of *Timon* in an interesting essay by Andor Gomme, in *Essays in Criticism*, IX, 2, April 1959.

II

I

I WISH to start this lecture by drawing your atten
tion to Professor H. D. F. Kitto's *Form and Meaning
in Drama*.[1] It would be almost an impertinence for me
to praise it, but I may say that even for a Greekless
reader it is a fascinating experience to see how a scholar
who is also a critic sets about his task of eliciting the
moral centre and the unifying pattern of plays by
Aeschylus and Sophocles. Now in this book Professor
Kitto has a long chapter on *Hamlet* that can be read
with profit by any student of Shakespeare, and I want
to use that chapter—both by way of agreement and
of disagreement—as a means of introducing my own
reflections on the play.

The great Greek tragedies, Professor Kitto insists,
are 'religious drama'—'a form of drama in which the
real focus is not the Tragic Hero', as conceived for
example by Aristotle, 'but the divine background'
(p. 231). Our attention is certainly demanded for the
figures on the stage, but it does not stop there; it goes
beyond them to a philosophic conception of the
general laws that govern human life, and it is these
laws that, with varying degrees of naturalism or of
departure from it, the action is designed to demonstrate. We do not say of the characters, How life-like
they are! We say, Yes this is indeed the way things

[1] Methuen, 1956

31

happen in the moral world. Now Hamlet also is
'religious drama', of which the artistic unity is lost 'if
we try to make the Tragic Hero the focus' (pp. 244-5).
The theme is evil, its contagion, and its inevitable self-
destruction—'evil breeding evil, and leading to ruin'
(p. 324). In the final scene 'we are made to feel that
Providence is working in the events; an eternal Law is
being exemplified: "There is a special providence in the
fall of a sparrow." . . . What is taking place is something like the working-out of Dikê'—or Law (p. 327).
As for Hamlet himself, what paralyses him is an over-
whelming sense of evil not only in Claudius or his
mother but in almost the whole world constituted by
the court of Denmark: his is 'a real paralysing despair
in the face of a life that has suddenly lost its meaning'
(p. 290). Weeds—the 'things rank and gross' in Denmark's unweeded garden—

> weeds can choke flowers. These weeds have choked
> Ophelia, and at last they choke Hamlet, because he
> could not do the coarse work of eradicating them.
> First, his comprehensive awareness of evil, reversing
> every habit of his mind, left him prostrate in anguish
> and apathy; then, the desire for vengeance being
> aroused, he missed everything by trying to encom-
> pass too much; finally, pursuing honour when it was
> nearly too late, he found it, but only in his own
> death. So finely poised, so brittle a nature as
> Hamlet's, is especially vulnerable to the destructive
> power of evil (pp. 327-8).

Now I feel sure that Professor Kitto is right about
the nature of Hamlet's paralysis; but I also think that
his development of the idea of the 'contagion' (p. 337)

suffered by Hamlet is not a full or adequate answer to the questions raised by the play. Is it enough to say that Hamlet 'feels himself being inexorably dragged down . . . to actions which, being free, he would condemn'—such as the murder of Rosencrantz and Guildenstern? (p. 320). Is it enough to say that 'Hamlet's "madness" was but the reflection of the evil with which he found himself surrounded, of which Claudius was the most prolific source' (p. 327)? Can we in short sum up the play as Kitto does towards the end of his essay?

In *Hamlet*, Shakespeare draws a complete character, not for the comparatively barren purpose of 'creating' a Hamlet for our admiration, but in order to show how he, like the others, is inevitably engulfed by the evil that has been set in motion, and how he himself becomes the cause of further ruin. The conception which unites these eight persons in one coherent catastrophe may be said to be this: evil, once started on its course, will so work as to attack and overthrow impartially the good and bad; and if the dramatist makes us feel, as he does, that a Providence is ordinant in all this, that, as with the Greeks, in his way of universalizing the particular event. (p. 330).

I think this is, at best, a partial summing-up; and I also think that there is some confusion that we should try to dissipate. Evil of course can 'overthrow' the good as well as the bad, in the sense that it can torture and kill them. But to the extent that they are 'engulfed' by it, as Hamlet is said to be engulfed —and this, in context, refers not to his happiness but

to his nature—to that extent they deviate from goodness. Kitto tells us that 'in Denmark, Hamlet's fineness
must necessarily suffer corruption' (p. 320). But why?
I cannot feel that 'contagion' is an adequate answer.
What I do feel is that the play prompts us to look much
more closely at the attitudes with which Hamlet
confronts his world and the gross evil in that world.

Now I want to insist that I admire Kitto's essay very
much. It is, to say the least, a fine example of a salutary
tendency of recent criticism to see Shakespeare's
tragedies as imaginative wholes rather than as dramatic
constructions designed to exhibit 'character', however
fascinating. And what gives the essay its value is not
only the acuteness of its specific analysis but its concern
with those moral and religious issues to which the
presentation of 'character' is strictly subordinate. But
if Shakespearean tragedy is 'religious drama' (for we
can apply this term to other plays besides *Hamlet*) in so
far as it is concerned not simply to draw the portrait of
an outstanding individual but to focus the fundamental
laws of human life, it is, I think, religious in a different
way from that defined in Kitto's account of Greek
tragedy. This, we are told, shows the working out of
inexorable laws. And so indeed does *Hamlet*—but with
this difference: we are required not only to *watch* the
august working out of the law which the dramatist's
understanding of spiritual and psychological truth
enables him to put before us; we are required to enter
imaginatively into the spiritual and psychological
states with which the given experience is confronted.
And this additional dimension—the dimension of
inwardness—forces us to be something other than

34

spectators. Kitto writes, 'we may say that both in the
Greek trilogy (the *Oresteia*) and in Shakespeare's play
the Tragic Hero, ultimately, is humanity itself; and
what humanity is suffering from, in *Hamlet*, is not a
specific evil, but Evil itself' (p. 335). Yes, in *Hamlet* the
preoccupation *is* with Evil itself, but this is presented
with a greater immediacy than Kitto's account, taken
as a whole, suggests. And when we attend to this—the
full imaginative effect—there is a timbre or quality that
perplexes us. Our perplexities centre on Hamlet, and
when we attend to them we find that Shakespeare is
not simply presenting the working out of Law, Dikê,
he is also—I think—questioning the perceiver.

II

And now, before coming directly to the play, I
wonder if I may take one more bearing on it with the
help of a book of a very different kind—the *De Con-
solatione Philosophiae* of Boethius, who, in Dante's words,
unmasks the deceitful world (*il mondo fallace*) to whoso
gives him good hearing, and whose thought had such
profound influence throughout the Middle Ages and
beyond. The *Consolation*, written in prison when
Boethius was awaiting death (524 A.D.), was one of the
main transmitters of pagan philosophy to the middle
ages—it was translated into English by, among others,
King Alfred and Chaucer—and in it may be found some
of the seminal ideas of medieval thought, such as the
naturalness of good, goodness as being, evil as mere
negation, evil as a perverted and unnatural attempt to
achieve the happiness that all men desire; for Boethius

as for so many after him, ignorance and passion are the causes of wrong choice, and vice is 'a sickness of the mind'. The book is not—as, knowing the circumstances of its composition, one might perhaps expect— a plea for stoic endurance; it is a sustained and varied demonstration of how a man may find and preserve his essential nature under the impact of great adversity and great perturbation. At the heart of it is the perception that man's essential nature cannot be satisfied by anything less than that goodness which is the desired health of the soul: being, the blessedness of virtue, and happiness are one and the same.

Now all this is nobly argued and, as I said, the book had an enormous influence in the Middle Ages and beyond. It was certainly well known in Shakespeare's day; Queen Elizabeth I translated it, and the current Loeb edition is substantially based on the translation of one, I. T., which first appeared in 1609. Whether Shakespeare did in fact read it I do not know, for although there are many passages and phrases in the *Consolation* which at once call to mind passages and phrases in Shakespeare's works—mainly, as it happens, in *Hamlet* but also in *King Lear*—these may have come down simply as part of the common stock of the age. There is however nothing to forbid the supposition that he had read the *Consolation*, and I want for the moment to play with the fancy that we can see him as he comes to the end of it. As he puts it down he says, 'This is a great and noble book, a book to return to and meditate on. It tells how a man may meet and rise above adversity, And yet . . . it is "philosophy", and there are more things in heaven and earth than philosophy can take official notice of: there's the whole turbulent living consciousness out of which such philosophy as we may achieve must draw its life. If I am to write my play about a man who is really cornered, really "tormented in this sea of fortune" as Boethius puts it, I've got to give not the abstract words for all that is over against him, but the whole oppressive feel of it. . . . And there's the complication of it all for the poor playwright. For if I make my Hamlet the central consciousness of the play, and try to show how his world *feels*—how indeed it smells—to him, then his feelings, the feelings that I imagine for him, will enter into the picture of the world that my play gives. Put it another way. In the very act of describing Hamlet's world as it feels to him in his own immediate consciousness, I have to describe Hamlet, to define that consciousness. That, though I have tackled something like it before, is a very pretty problem indeed. I don't think that my young man will answer the questions that his world, my play, will force upon him, though he may perhaps in his very failure point the way to an answer . . . And there's another challenge too. This book of Boethius's—it gives us great and noble thoughts; what it doesn't give, what it isn't intended to give, is all that lies behind thought in the obscurer regions of the soul where thought begins. One day I may be able to show how real thinking in this region— the region of the great questions—depends on the feelings and the imagination. . . . I'll show a man feeling his way through, and seeing feelingly. . . .'

King Lear, however, is still some way ahead, and *Hamlet* is our present concern. Let us turn to the play.

III

What—if we refuse to intellectualize too much, to follow clues as in a detective story, to engage in the fascinating sport of character dissection—what is the main imaginative impact that the play makes upon us? As Professor C. S. Lewis insisted in his British Academy Lecture, *'Hamlet': the Prince or the Poem?* (1942), *Hamlet* is not about a man whose character is an enigma to be unravelled, it is about a man who suffers a certain kind of experience, and the man and the experience go together. It is not about a man who could not make up his mind, or a man with peculiarly puzzling reasons for refusing to act; it is a play about death and—to use for the moment a wide and loosely defining phrase—it is a play about corruption. When we are really living through the experience both are present to our consciousness under wide-ranging aspects: death as mere physical fact and as metaphysical terror; corruption as obtuseness, gross sensuality and deliberate contrived evil. I think this is obvious enough, but let us pause for a moment to make it vivid to our minds. And since Hamlet's consciousness, which dominates so much of the play, will shortly be the main object of our consideration, let us for a moment consider the action of the play, so far as possible, as directly presented, without reference to what Hamlet himself may say about it.

It is well known how, right at the start of each of his tragedies, Shakespeare establishes the 'atmosphere'—something that is not just a vaguely effective background but an integral part of the play's structure of meanings. In *Hamlet*, with the usual effective economy of means, we are made aware of a cold darkness that makes men 'sick at heart'. In the surrounding stillness ('not a mouse stirring') men's voices ring out sharply and with subdued apprehension. In this 'dead vast'—vacancy, void, emptiness—'and middle of the night', when Bernardo points to the 'star that's westward from the pole', and speaks of 'the bell then beating one', there is something of that sense of a surrounding non-human that reverberates from the steeples in Robert Frost's 'I will sing you One-O':

> In that grave One
> They spoke of the sun
> And moon and stars,
> Saturn and Mars . . .

In that setting—which will shortly contrast so strongly with the light and pomp and self-important complacency of King Claudius's court—we first hear of, then see, a dead man's ghost. It is of course important not to rewrite Shakespeare's plays for him but to follow his lead as closely as we may. But the emphasis here is indeed Shakespeare's. As C. S. Lewis says, 'The Hamlet formula, so to speak, is not "a man who has to avenge his father", but "a man who has been given a task by a ghost" '. And he adds that whereas in the other tragedies plenty of people are concerned with dying, 'no one thinks, in these plays, of being dead. In *Hamlet* we are kept thinking about it all the time, whether in terms of the soul's destiny or of the body's.' The dead man's ghost is the mainspring of the action, which involves, finally, eight other deaths. Of that original death the memory is indeed 'green', from the first

39

scene, through the re-enactment of the murder by the Players, to the rhetorical question of Fortinbras at the end,

> O proud Death!
> What feast is toward in thine eternal cell . . .?

And it is quite early offered as an example of obvious and inescapable mortality: 'your father lost a father, That father lost, lost his'; it is 'as common As any the most vulgar thing to sense'; the 'common theme' 'is death of fathers', and reason

> still hath cried,
> From the first corse [ironically Abel's] till he that
> died to-day,
> 'This must be so'.

From this until the Play scene the theme is mainly expressed by Hamlet, but from the killing of Polonius the presence of death is very close indeed. Polonius, interred 'in hugger-mugger', is 'compounded with dust'; death shares with sex the burden of Ophelia's mad songs; there is the long elegiac description of her drowning. Above all, there is Act V, scene i—the scene with the grave-diggers. Here, as so often in Shakespeare, a dominant theme entwined in a complex action is for a short space given full and exclusive prominence.

> What is he that builds stronger than either the mason, the shipwright, or the carpenter? . . . a gravemaker; the houses that he makes last till doomsday.

To the accompaniment of snatches of song, in which love gives way to death, the Clown throws up the skulls that Hamlet comments on: politician, courtier,

lawyer, tanner, fine lady, jester, Caesar, Alexander—
not one can escape this fate. The moral is enforced
with the simplification of a *danse macabre*:

> Now get you to my lady's chamber, and tell her,
> let her paint an inch thick, to this favour she must
>   come; make her laugh at that.

On the one hand, then, is death, on the other is life
lived with a peculiarly crude vigour of self-assertion.
In the world that Hamlet confronts, men mostly, as
the phrase goes, know what they want—plenty to eat
and drink, sexual satisfaction, and power—and they
see that they get it, pursuing their limited aims with
a gross complacence, fat weeds that rot themselves in
ease on the wharf of oblivion. At this stage there is no
need to describe in detail the forms of corruption of
that Denmark in which any decent man would feel
himself in prison. There is murder, of course, but even
before we know that Claudius is a murderer, it is clear
that on his first appearance we are intended to register
something repulsive. His very first speech is a masterly
example of 'the distillation of personality into style'.

> Though yet of Hamlet our dear brother's death
> The memory be green, and that it us befitted
> To bear our hearts in grief and our whole kingdom
> To be contracted in one brow of woe,
> Yet so far hath discretion fought with nature
> That we with wisest sorrow think on him,
> Together with remembrance of ourselves . . .

That, surely, is the tone and accent of Milton's Belial;
we need know nothing of Claudius's previous activities

to react to those unctuous verse rhythms with some such comment as 'Slimy beast!'. Neither the King's practical efficiency in dealing with the public affairs of his kingdom, nor his ostensible kindness towards his nephew, can wipe out that first impression. This is the man whose accession to the throne, and whose indecently hasty—and, in an Elizabethan view, incestuous—marriage with his dead brother's wife has been 'freely' endorsed by the 'better wisdoms' of the Council. In the whole Court of Denmark there is no one, Hamlet apart, to utter a breath of criticism. How should there be? The ethos of the place—so we are told, or directly shown—is made up of coarse pleasures—

> This heavy-headed revel east and west
> Makes us traduced and tax'd of other nations;
> They clepe us drunkards, and with swinish phrase
> Soil our addition;

it is made up of moral obtuseness (Polonius), sycophancy (Rosencrantz and Guildenstern), base and treacherous plotting (Laertes) and—since Shakespeare didn't introduce Osric at the climax of the tragedy for the sake of a little harmless fun—brainless triviality. This is the world that revolves round the middle-aged sensuality of Claudius and Gertrude. 'Something is rotten in the state of Denmark'; and if anyone should be in any doubt of the completeness with which corruption permeates that state, I suggest, before his next re-reading, a glance at Professor Kitto's chapter. 'What humanity is suffering from, in *Hamlet*, is not a specific evil, but Evil itself.'

Now it is well known that some other plays of this period exhibit, with an almost obsessive insistence, death and corruption—Webster's tragedies, for example. But when we have finished *The White Devil* or *The Duchess of Malfi*, we are likely to find ourselves in some perplexity concerning what it is all about. What is the point of it? When we have finished reading *Hamlet* we have at least a fair idea of what it is about. The point is not a display of accumulated horrors; it is the effect of these on a particular kind of consciousness. It is this that is the centre of interest, and the question that is so often pursued, almost, as it were, in isolation from the full imaginative effect, Why does Hamlet delay? is entirely subordinate to the wider and more inclusive question: What is the impact on Hamlet's consciousness of the world with which he has to deal? If, at this point, I may risk a bald anticipatory summary of what must be dealt with at more length, I would say this: that Hamlet, in his confrontation of this world, feels himself paralysed because an exclusive concentration on evil, or—say—something in the manner of the concentration, is itself corrupting.

> The finished man among his enemies?—
> How in the name of Heaven can he escape
> That defiling and disfigured shape
> The mirror of malicious eyes
> Casts upon his eyes until at last
> He thinks that shape must be his shape?
> And what's the good of an escape
> If honour find him in the wintry blast?

That, from Yeats's 'A Dialogue of Self and Soul', is in no sense a summing-up of *Hamlet*; but it does, I think,

43

suggest something of the play's central concern. 'The
characters', if I may quote C. S. Lewis again, 'are all
watching one another, forming theories about one
another, listening, contriving, full of anxiety. The
world of *Hamlet* is a world where one has lost one's
way. The Prince also has no doubt lost his. . . .' It is
because attention is centred so continuously on this
losing of the way by a character who in so many and
such obvious ways is superior to those who surround
him, that the play is so radical an examination of the
problem of consciousness, of self-identity. That is why
the line that everyone thinks of in connexion with this
play—though we all quarrel about its meaning—is, 'To
be, or not to be, that is the question . . .'

IV

The climax of the first movement of the play—that
is, of Act I—is Hamlet's encounter with the Ghost. It
is important that we should get clear with ourselves
how we are intended to take it. At first it seems that
Shakespeare is careful to keep the status of the Ghost
more or less neutral. The first we hear of it is Marcellus's
'What, has this thing appear'd again to-night?' As a
ghost, it is of course a 'dreaded sight', a 'portentous
figure', but it is also, simply, 'this apparition', 'illusion', 'this present object'. When Horatio tells Hamlet
what has happened, it is 'a figure like your father' and
'the apparition'. None of this provides any very clear
answer to the question that an audience is likely to ask
—What sort of a ghost is this? Is it good or bad? There
are however some suggestive tonings. The Ghost,

44

though 'majestical', starts 'like a guilty thing' when the cock crows, and we are told that this is because the bird's 'lofty and shrill-sounding throat' awakes 'the god of day', but dismisses 'to his confine' 'the extravagant and erring spirit'. Both these adjectives may mean no more than wandering out of bounds or straying, but the immediately following lines suggest rather more than this.

> It faded on the crowing of the cock.
> Some say that ever 'gainst that season comes
> Wherein our Saviour's birth is celebrated,
> The bird of dawning singeth all night long;
> And then, they say, no spirit dare stir abroad;
> The nights are wholesome; then no planets strike,
> No fairy takes, nor witch hath power to charm,
> So hallow'd and so gracious is that time.

Now I cannot believe that these lines were put in for the sake of an incidental bit of 'poetry'—no more than I could believe it of the temple-haunting martlets passage in *Macbeth*, which similarly contrasts so markedly with the thick and oppressive atmosphere that permeates most of the play. Here, in the passage before us, not only is Christmas night wholesome, hallowed and gracious, because various malign influences are as powerless to act as spirits such as this are to stir abroad, the limpid freshness of the verse emphasizes an accepted Christianity ('our Saviour's birth') which, it seems in place to remark, is directly opposed to the code of revenge. Ah but, we may be told, in *Hamlet* Shakespeare is using the conventions of the revenge play, in which quite different assumptions about the duty of revenge prevail. This has always seemed to me a very rum argument indeed. Shakespeare may use various dramatic conventions—such as the foreshortening of time or the impenetrability of disguise—when they suit his purpose; but he never—what great poet could? —allows convention to shape his essential matter. I cannot believe that the poet who was going on to write *Measure for Measure* (perhaps his next play), which is about forgiveness, who was going on to create the figure of Cordelia, and to write those plays of which a main part of the burden is that 'the rarer action is in virtue than in vengeance'—I cannot believe that such a poet could temporarily waive his deepest ethical convictions for the sake of an exciting dramatic effect. It is almost like believing that Dante, for a canto or two, could change his ground and write approvingly, say, of the enemies of the Empire. If this ghost turns out to be one who clamours for revenge, then we have every reason to suppose that Shakespeare entertained some grave doubts about him.

This, however, is to anticipate. All we can say when the first scene ends is that the play has given us reason to be suspicious of the Ghost. When in scene iv it appears to Hamlet himself, his address to it still allows for alternative possibilities:

Be thou a spirit of health, or goblin damned,
Bring with thee airs from heaven, or blasts from hell,
Be thy intents wicked, or charitable . . .

but what is emphasized at the end of this same speech is that for the 'dead corse' to revisit 'the glimpses of the moon' is to make night 'hideous'; it is also

So horridly to shake our disposition
With thoughts beyond the reaches of our souls.

There follows the—surely choric—warning of Horatio:

> What if it tempt you toward the flood, my lord,
> Or to the dreadful summit of the cliff
> That beetles o'er his base into the sea,
> And there assume some other horrible form,
> Which might deprive your sovereignty of reason
> And draw you into madness? think of it;
> The very place puts toys of desperation,
> Without more motive, into every brain
> That looks so many fathoms to the sea
> And hears it roar beneath.

No one, I suppose, can read these lines without recalling the description, in *King Lear*, of that Dover cliff over which Gloucester thinks to peer with his sightless eyes—a scene which, in the parallel progress of the two old men, reminds us of how Lear too had peered into the abyss that opened up within, for 'the mind, mind has mountains; cliffs of fall Frightful, sheer, no-man-fathomed'. Edgar, evoking the scene, declares, 'I'll look no more, Lest my brain turn', and Horatio—

> The very place puts toys of desperation,
> Without more motive, into every brain. . . .

'Desperation', moreover, like 'desperate' a few lines later ('He waxes desperate with imagination'), is a far stronger word than, say, 'recklessness' (it is related to 'despair'), and I think we may say that the speech as a whole gives us an unambiguous clue: the Ghost is tempting Hamlet to gaze with fascinated horror at an abyss of evil.

Now the evil is real enough: that also has been established in Act I, and there is certainly nothing

unnatural in the violence of Hamlet's recoil from it—
'O! that this too too sullied flesh would melt. . . .' The
question is how Hamlet will deal with this world—
deal with it not only in action, but *within himself*. The
Ghost's demand, when the two are finally confronted
alone, is for an exclusive concentration on it, and it is
to that demand that Hamlet gives himself up.

> Remember thee?
> Yea, from the table of my memory
> I'll wipe away all trivial fond records,
> All saws of books, all forms, all pressures past,
> That youth and observation copied there;
> And thy commandment all alone shall live
> Within the book and volume of my brain,
> Unmix'd with baser matter.

There is a terrible significance in that repeated 'all', for
what it means is that Hamlet does not merely see the
evil about him, does not merely react to it with loathing and rejection, he allows his vision to activate
something within himself—say, if you like, his own
feeling of corruption—and so to produce that state of
near paralysis that so perplexes him.

not well
supported!

Ref p. 43

We can accept the argument
as a possible consequence
an excellent supporting
but not necessarily as
a fact!

III

I

THE point of view that I am putting forward is that what we have in *Hamlet*—as in *Othello* and, less successfully, in *Timon*—is the exploration and implicit criticism of a particular state of mind or consciousness. It is an extremely complex state of mind, in which reason and emotion, attitudes towards the self and towards other persons and the world at large, are revealed both directly and through a series of encounters; and our business is to see how the different ingredients (so to speak) are related in such a way that a particular judgment or assessment of experience is precipitated. Since that remark sounds formal and moralistic let me add two qualifying statements. The first is that what we have to do with is not a state of mind that can be adequately described in terms of abstract reason. As J. I. M. Stewart has said, in *Character and Motive in Shakespeare*:

It is . . . necessary to recognise that the poetic drama, like myth, is part-based upon an awareness, largely intuitive, of the recesses of human passion and motive. . . . Of just what Shakespeare brings from beyond this portal [of the depths of the mind], and how, we often can achieve little conceptual grasp; and often therefore the logical and unkindled mind finds difficulties which it labels as faults and attributes to the depravity of Shakespeare's audience

D   49

or what it wills. But what the intellect finds arbitrary the imagination may accept and respond to, for when we read imaginatively or poetically we share the dramatist's penetration for a while and deep is calling to deep.

That, I think, is well said. Hamlet's state of mind, the Hamlet consciousness, is revealed not only at the level of formulable motive, but in its obscure depths; and it is revealed through the poetry. In the second place, the judgment of which I spoke is not a matter of formal approval or condemnation of a dramatic figure conceived as a real person. No doubt it is partly that; but essentially it is part of an imaginative apprehension of life in which, with the whole force of our personality ('judgment ever awake and steady self-possession combined with enthusiasm and feeling profound or vehement'), we try to see fundamental aspects of human life in their true status and relationships. And what we judge, in this sense, is not someone 'out there', but potentialities of our own being.

In the particular complex of feelings and attitudes that constitute the Hamlet consciousness it is not easy to separate causes and effects, but I think that most people would agree that what is emphasized from the opening scenes is a movement of recoil and disgust of a peculiar intensity. Whether this negative emotion is, as T. S. Eliot once claimed, 'in excess of the facts as they appear' is a question that may be waived for the moment. What is indisputable is that for the greater part of the play it is stronger than any counterbalancing movements of positive and outgoing life. And the determining moment, when this imbalance is accepted as a kind of compulsion is, as we saw in the last lecture, the encounter with the Ghost. When Hamlet swears to 'remember'—with such ominous repetition of the word—he commits himself to a passion that has all the exclusiveness of an infatuation.

> Remember thee?
> Ay, thou poor ghost, while memory holds a seat
> In this distracted globe. Remember thee?
> Yea, from the table of my memory
> I'll wipe away all trivial fond records,
> All saws of books, all forms, all pressures past,
> That youth and observation copied there;
> And thy commandment all alone shall live
> Within the book and volume of my brain,
> Unmix'd with baser matter.

There is, I remarked, a terrible significance in that *all*. Now Hamlet's exclusive concentration upon things rank and gross and his consequent recoil from life as a whole determine his attitude to death, which also is purely one of negation. Some contrasts may help us here. When T. S. Eliot's *Little Gidding* was first published a notable review of that poem, by D. W. Harding, appeared in *Scrutiny* (XI, 3, 1943). Speaking of the way in which a sense of spiritual values can reveal a significant pattern in a life which must otherwise appear meaningless and fragmentary, Harding remarked of the closing sections of the poem:

One effect of this view of time and experience is to rob the moment of death of any over-significance we may have given it. For the humanist of Section II life trails off just because it can't manage to endure. For the man convinced of spiritual values life is a coherent pattern in which the ending has its due place and, because it is part of a pattern, itself leads into the beginning. An over-strong terror of death is often one expression of the fear of living, for death is one of the life-processes that seem too terrifying to be borne. In examining one means of becoming reconciled to death, Mr. Eliot can show us life, too, made bearable, unfrightening, positively inviting: 'With the drawing of this Love and the voice of this Calling'.

'An over-strong terror of death is often one expression of the fear of living.' There is of course an instinctive recoil from dying, expressed magnificently by Shakespeare in Claudio's outburst—'Aye, but to die, and go we know not where'—in *Measure for Measure*; but we are speaking now of settled attitudes, and I think it is obvious that strong, unfrightened and affirmative attitudes to death can only exist as part of strong, unfrightened and affirmative attitudes to living. We could cite the superb closing pages of the Second Part of *The Pilgrim's Progress* (of which I remember F. R. Leavis once remarking to me that no civilization could long endure that did not incorporate in itself some comparable affirmative attitudes); but perhaps here Shakespeare is our most relevant witness, and we may recall how in *The Tempest* the sense of wonder and freshness goes with a serene acceptance of the full human condition; indeed that speech in which Prospero speaks of the transience of all things human begins,

You do look, my son, in a moved sort,
As if you were dismay'd; be cheerful, sir.

Now for Hamlet, on the other hand, death is mere negation; but at the same time he is fascinated by it, fascinated not merely by 'the dread of something after death', but by the whole process of earthly corruption, as in the long brooding on the skulls in the churchyard, culminating in the gratuitous fantasy of the progress of Alexander:

> To what base uses we may return, Horatio! Why may not imagination trace the noble dust of Alexander, till he find it stopping a bung-hole?

To which, you remember, Horatio replies, ''Twere to consider too curiously, to consider so'; but Hamlet does not heed him. Certainly the facts that Hamlet dwells on here, as he had dwelt on them in connexion with the death of Polonius, are facts that have to be assimilated somehow, but it is the tone and manner that are betraying:

> —Now, Hamlet, where's Polonius?
> —At supper . . . Not where he eats, but where he is eaten; a certain convocation of politic worms are e'en at him. Your worm is your only emperor for diet; we fat all creatures else to fat us, and we fat ourselves for maggots . . .

society too !

and again:

> —Dost thou think Alexander looked o' this fashion i' the earth?
> —E'en so.
> —And smelt so? pah!

It need cause no surprise that these attitudes of fascinated revulsion combine with a regressive longing for the death that, from another point of view, appears so repulsive. We shall shortly have occasion to look at the 'To be, or not to be' soliloquy in some detail. Here I would simply call attention to the way in which it expresses this basic aspect of Hamlet's attitude to death. The speech (if I may make use of what I have written elsewhere) 'is built up on two contrasted sets of metaphors. Life, "this mortal coil", is at best something which hampers and impedes, imposing "fardels" under which we "grunt and sweat"; "the slings and arrows of outrageous fortune", "the thousand natural shocks", and "the whips and scorns of time" present it as an actively hostile force; and in "a sea of troubles" the power that it has to inflict pain is felt as continuous and irresistible like the sea. Death, on the other hand, is presented simply as a relaxing of tension and an abandonment of the struggle. The reiterated "sleep", the soothing "quietus", and the smooth and weighted "consummation", make plain why death is so ardently desired by a spirit which, whether "suffering" or "opposing", feels itself continually on the defensive against a world conceived as entirely hostile.' The essay from which I am quoting I have come to feel as decidedly fragmentary and provisional, but I see no reason to retract the conclusion that what we have here is a quality of moral relaxation, a desire to lapse *back* from the level of adult consciousness. What has to be added is that Hamlet finally accepts death in words of a peculiarly haunting quality to which we shall return; but it is from the standpoint of a life that has been largely emptied of significance.

II

[Hamlet is a man who in the face of life and of death can make no affirmation, and it may well be that this irresolution—which goes far deeper than irresolution about the performance of a specific act—this fundamental doubt, explains the great appeal of the play in modern times.] The point has been made by D. G. James in *The Dream of Learning*. Shakespeare's play, he says, 'is an image of modernity, of the soul without clear belief losing its way, and bringing itself and others to great distress and finally to disaster'; it is 'a tragedy not of excessive thought but of defeated thought', and Hamlet himself is 'a man caught in ethical and metaphysical uncertainties'. Now I am sure that Mr. James is right in emphasizing the element of scepticism in Hamlet's make-up—the weighing of alternative possibilities in such a way as to make choice between them virtually impossible; and I sympathize with his wish 'to elevate Hamlet's intellectual distresses to an equality in importance with his emotional state', for 'the strength of the emotional shock he has suffered is equalled by the weakness of his mind in the face of difficult moral and metaphysical issues. Hamlet was, after all, an intellectual.' But at the same time I feel that the play incites us to a closer examination of the intimate and complex relationship of thought and feeling, of intellectual bafflement and certain aspects of the emotional life; in the play before us the dominant emotions are activated by certain specific shocks but they cannot be attributed solely to these.

In an essay called *Hamlet and Don Quixote* Ivan

Turgenev took up this very question of Hamlet's scepticism, but instead of regarding it as a purely intellectual matter he related it to central attitudes of the self, to a certain moral inadequacy.

> Hamlet (he says) is, beyond all things else, analysis and egoism, scepticism personified.
>
> He lives only to himself. He is an egoist, and as such can have no faith in himself; for no man can have faith save in that which is outside self and above self.
>
> None the less Hamlet clings tenaciously to this 'I', this self in which he has no faith. It is a centre to which he constantly returns because he finds that in this world there is nothing to which he can cleave with all his soul.
>
> A sceptic, Hamlet is preoccupied with his own personality; but he ponders its strategical situation, not its duties.[1]

In other words, Hamlet is one of those in whom 'the "I" in the individual' preponderates, not 'something outside the "I"', which the individual prefers to the "I"'. Now I think that this also is true, but again, taken in isolation, it does not quite do justice to the imaginative facts as we know them; for what it ignores is the pain and the passion—the genuine pain of loss and the genuine passion of revulsion against what is really evil. Max Plowman perhaps, in an essay called 'Some Values in *Hamlet*' (reprinted in *The Right to*

---

[1] I quote from the translation by Robert Nichols (London: Henderson, 1930). I was reminded of the existence of Turgenev's little known essay by the reference in Miss Rebecca West's *The Court and the Castle: the Interaction of Political and Religious Ideas in Imaginative Literature*: in the chapters on *Hamlet* Miss West has some interesting things to say about current misconceptions of the play.

Live) brings us nearer the mark when he speaks of Hamlet as one who has risen above the level of the merely instinctive—the level at which most of those who surround him live, and at which revenge is an obvious duty—but who has not risen to full and adequate consciousness.

> For as we come to objective consciousness, we realize that no one lives to himself: we know, in fact, that life consists in the interplay of subject and object, and that the completely isolated person can only be said to exist; for to be completely isolated is to lack intercourse with anything outside the self.

Hamlet, on the other hand, is in the intermediate state of self-consciousness, 'the most unlovable of all conditions': 'Hamlet is self-conscious man in an unconscious world'; what he suffers from is 'a fixation of self-consciousness'. The point, you see, is very close to that made by Turgenev. But there is this difference: Max Plowman sees Hamlet's state as one phase in a development that is not peculiar to any one individual; however far Hamlet goes astray he starts from a point through which everyone—or almost everyone—must pass who is to rise above the instinctive and unself-knowing to that state of genuine being for which one name is consciousness.

I think we shall not be far wrong if, in seeking to account for Hamlet's paralysis, his inability to affirm, we give special prominence to his isolation and self-consciousness. Now consciousness, as distinguished from Hamlet's self-consciousness, is dependent upon love and relationship, and the name that Blake gave to consciousness, as Max Plowman remarks in this same essay, is the Imagination. Hamlet, for all his ranging mind and his nervous susceptibility, is not in this sense imaginative; in Blakean terms he is in the power of his Spectre.

> Each Man is in his Spectre's power
> Untill the arrival of that hour,
> When his Humanity awake
> And cast his own Spectre into the Lake.

These lines occur in the Rossetti MS. Looking up other instances of 'Spectre' in the Index to the edition of the Prophetic Writings by Sloss and Wallis, I found (what I had not noticed before) that Blake also used them in *Jerusalem*: in the drawing showing Albion in despair (Plate 41) they are engraved in reverse on the stone at the feet of the seated bowed figure, his face covered by his hands; and it is not irrelevant to our present concerns to notice that the passage immediately following this illustration begins,

> Thus Albion sat, studious of others in his pale disease,
> Brooding on evil . . .

I hope you will not misunderstand me. I do not think that Shakespeare wrote *Hamlet* as an esoteric commentary on Blake's Prophetic Books, or that Hamlet's Ghost is to be identified with Blake's Spectre. It is simply that both poets had some comparable insights, and the one may be used to bring out the meaning of the other. Blake's Spectre is the rationalizing faculty, self-centred and moralistic, working in isolation from the other powers and potentialities of the mind. Unless redeemed by Los, the Imagination, in dealing with the self and with others it can only criticize and accuse, creating around itself what Wordsworth was to call 'a universe of death.'

Hamlet, 'studious of others in his pale disease, Brooding on evil,' is, in this sense, in the power of his Spectre. He is indeed, as Mr James and many others have insisted, an intellectual, a man given to reason and reflection. But what Shakespeare is bringing in question in this play is what it means to be an intellectual in any but a sterile sense, the conditions on which this capability can be indeed 'god-like'. Hamlet's intellectuality, the working of his mind, is largely at the service of attitudes of rejection and disgust that are indiscriminate in their working. Let me repeat what I have said before: the Denmark of this play is indeed an unweeded garden; there are facts enough to justify almost everything Hamlet says about this world; but what we have to take note of is not only what he says but a particular vibration in the saying. We can define this in relation to his self-disgust, his spreading sexual nausea, and his condemnation of others.

III

When Hamlet first reveals himself in soliloquy it is in terms of a revulsion for which the preceding court scene has in some measure prepared us.

O! that this too too sullied flesh would melt,
Thaw and resolve itself into a dew . . .

His flesh is sullied because it is the flesh of a woman who, in a matter of weeks from the death of her first husband, has married her husband's brother: 'a beast, that wants discourse of reason, Would have mourn'd longer'; she is moreover infatuated with a man who clearly has some of the qualities of the 'satyr' that Hamlet attributes to him. These are données of the case, and it need occasion no surprise when Hamlet declares that 'virtue cannot so inoculate our old stock but we shall relish of it'. This sense of being tainted is both explicable and natural, but Shakespeare is careful to show us that there is more than this involved in Hamlet's bitter judgment on himself. The disgust with the self that we must all at some time feel, for whatever cause, changes its quality when it is used to shock and damage, as Hamlet uses it to damage his dawning relationship with Ophelia.

> *Hamlet.* . . . if you be honest and fair, your honesty should admit no discourse to your beauty.
>
> *Ophelia.* Could beauty, my lord, have better commerce than with honesty?
>
> *Hamlet.* Ay, truly; for the power of beauty will sooner transform honesty from what it is to a bawd than the force of honesty can translate beauty into his likeness; this was sometime a paradox, but now the time gives it proof. I did love you once.
>
> *Ophelia.* Indeed, my lord, you made me believe so.
>
> *Hamlet.* You should not have believed me; for virtue cannot so inoculate our old stock but we shall relish of it; I loved you not.

Ophelia. I was the more deceived.

Hamlet. Get thee to a nunnery; why wouldst thou be a breeder of sinners? I am myself indifferent honest; but yet I could accuse me of such things that it were better my mother had not borne me. I am very proud, revengeful, ambitious; with more offences at my beck than I have thoughts to put them in, imagination to give them shape, or time to act them in. What should such fellows as I do crawling between heaven and earth? We are arrant knaves all; believe none of us. Go thy ways to a nunnery.

We may for the moment leave on one side the question of what Hamlet, in this and similar passages, is doing to another's consciousness—driving a wedge into it so that it too must inevitably suffer—though that Shakespeare was not indifferent to it we know from Ophelia's madness and her—apparently half-sought—death. But if we ask whether what Hamlet says or implies about himself is mature self-knowledge or, as Turgenev suggests, mere self-flagellation, I do not think that the answer can be in any doubt. 'I am very proud, revengeful, ambitious; with more offences at my beck than I have thoughts to put them in, imagination to give them shape, or time to act them in.' This, it has been said, 'sounds very terrible, but considered carefully it amounts to nothing'. What it means, it seems to me, is that Hamlet is in a state of panic recoil not only from sex but from those aggressions and self-assertive drives that sooner or later we have to come to terms with and put to constructive use. Many of Shakespeare's characters, it is true, are constrained to take stock of things

61

within of which they are bitterly ashamed. There is, for example, Lear:

> Poor naked wretches, whereso'er you are,
> That bide the pelting of this pitiless storm,
> How shall your houseless heads and unfed sides,
> Your loop'd and window'd raggedness, defend you
> From seasons such as this? O! I have ta'en
> Too little care of this. Take physic, pomp . . .

Or there is Posthumus, in prison and awaiting death:

> My conscience, thou are fetter'd
> More than my shanks and wrists; you good gods,
> give me
> The penitent instrument to pick that bolt;
> Then, free for ever! Is't enough I am sorry?
> So children temporal fathers do appease;
> Gods are more full of mercy. Must I repent?
> I cannot do it better than in gyves,
> Desir'd more than constrained; to satisfy,
> If of my freedom 'tis the main part, take
> No stricter render of me than my all . . .
> . . . and so, great powers,
> If you will take this audit, take this life,
> And cancel these cold bonds. O Imogen!
> I'll speak to thee in silence.

To say that there is an absolute difference of tone and intention between these self-communings and anything that Hamlet may say by way of self-condemnation is to comment on the obvious. When indeed he has anything real to repent of, his self-exculpatory manner suggests something like obliviousness to what he has done. Of the murder of Polonius:

> For this same lord,
> I do repent; but heaven hath pleased it so,
> To punish me with this, and this with me,
> That I must be their scourge and minister . . .

—to be followed shortly by 'I'll lug the guts into the neighbour room'. Of his unseemly ranting in Ophelia's grave with Laertes, whose father he has killed, and for whose sister's death he is at least in part to blame:

> What I have done,
> That might your nature, honour, and exception
> Roughly awake, I here proclaim was madness.
> Was't Hamlet wrong'd Laertes? Never Hamlet;
> If Hamlet from himself be ta'en away,
> And when he's not himself does wrong Laertes,
> Then Hamlet does it not; Hamlet denies it.
> Who does it then? His madness; if't be so,
> Hamlet is of the faction that is wrong'd;
> His madness is poor Hamlet's enemy.

One can hardly resist the feeling that some of the energy that Hamlet expends in unpacking his heart with words might more profitably have been directed —and with more humility—towards a stricter accounting of his share in the harm done to others.

It is much the same with his sexual insistence. Grant that he is deeply wounded—as who would not be?— by his mother's conduct:

> why, she would hang on him [her first husband]
> As if increase of appetite had grown
> By what it fed on . . .

> O, most wicked speed, to post
> With such dexterity to incestuous sheets!

63

Rebellious hell,
If thou canst mutine in a matron's bones,
To flaming youth let virtue be as wax
And melt in her own fire . . .

Grant this, and it still does not excuse his obscenity towards Ophelia—Ophelia whom he had said he loved, and she believed him—and it would not excuse it even if we were to accept Professor Dover Wilson's shift of a stage direction in II. ii. which makes Hamlet suspect her as a willing decoy of Claudius and Polonius. What he says to her in the 'get thee to a nunnery' scene and in the play scene can only be described in D. H. Lawrence's terms as 'doing dirt on sex'. But Hamlet was shocked by the revelation of the power of sex? Yes indeed, as an adolescent may well be horrified and frightened when the revelation of dangerous powers within comes as part of a traumatic experience. But Hamlet was not in years an adolescent; he was, as Shakespeare tells us, a man of thirty. As for his too vivid picturing of his mother's life with Claudius—

Not this, by no means, that I bid you do;
Let the bloat king tempt you again to bed;
Pinch wanton on your cheek; call you his mouse;
And let him, for a pair of reechy kisses,
Or paddling in your neck with his damn'd fingers,
Make you to ravel all this matter out . . .

—there is enough, here and elsewhere, to give plausibility to the psycho-analytic speculations of Dr. Ernest Jones.

I am of course aware that what Hamlet says to his mother in the Closet scene may be regarded as part of a necessary and proper attempt to break the alliance between her and the smiling murderer; but through it all runs the impure streak of the indulgence of an obsessive passion.

> Come, come, and sit you down; you shall not budge;
> You go not till I set you up a glass
> Where you may see the inmost part of you.

If with genuine, even with passionate, concern, you want to help someone in great need, someone in desperate ignorance of his true condition, do you, I wonder, say, 'This is what you are: see how ugly you look'? Well, perhaps you may; but certainly not in such a way that you seem about to make an aggressive attack. The Queen's immediate reaction, which acts as a stage direction indicating Hamlet's whole bearing, is, 'What wilt thou do? thou wilt not murder me? Help, help, ho!' Perhaps we may again invoke Lear, who as he comes to see more and more clearly the evil in the world, is also constrained to speak words of passionate denunciation: the difference, from the point of view of our present concern, is that these, like Lear's 'burning shame', have an almost impersonal intensity. Hamlet, in his denunciations, is never free of himself, never centres entirely on the matter in hand or the person before him.

Hamlet, in short, is fascinated by what he condemns. His emotions circle endlessly, but find no direction. And it is because of the impurity and indiscriminateness of his rejections that, brief moments of friendship and respite apart, he takes refuge in postures. There is a further point to be made here. I do not remember seeing the question asked, but why, on the success of the Gonzago play, does Hamlet call for the recorders?

> Ah, ha! Come, some music! come, the recorders!—
> For if the king like not the comedy,
> Why then, belike,—he likes it not, perdy.
> Come, some music!

True, Shakespeare knew that the recorders would be needed for the scene with Rosencrantz and Guildenstern, but this can hardly affect the reason imputed to Hamlet. The answer surely can only be that Hamlet intends the players to finish off the evening with a concert which Claudius will hear, thus keeping him in suspense and leaving the initiative of action to him: it will be one more *arranged scene*, and thus in line with Hamlet's habitual tendency to make everything, even what he deeply feels, into a matter of play-acting. Again and again intrinsic values, direct relations, are neglected whilst he tries out various roles before a real or imagined audience. He dramatizes his melancholy—for he insists on his suit of inky black even whilst denying its importance—just as he dramatizes his love and his fall from love and his very grief at Ophelia's death; his jests and asides imply an approving audience 'in the know' and ready to take the point; he is fascinated by the business of acting (and highly intelligent about it), and he falls naturally into figures of speech suggested by the theatre—'make mouths at the invisible event', 'Who calls me villain? breaks my pate across?' etc. Before the last scene the note of sincerity is found in few places except some of the soliloquies and the intimate exchanges with Horatio.

IV

Now to say that Hamlet adopts histrionic, even at times melodramatic, postures is to bring into view another matter of central importance—that is, the static quality of Hamlet's consciousness. It is not for nothing that the popular conception is that this is a play about delay. Delay in the action, that is in the carrying out of Hamlet's strategy against the King, can of course be explained: he had to find out if the Ghost was telling the truth about the murder, and so on. But the fact remains that one of the most powerful imaginative effects is of a sense of paralysis. Hamlet feels, and we are made to feel, that he is 'stuck', as we say on more homely occasions.

> Sure he that made us with such large discourse,
> Looking before and after, gave us not
> That capability and god-like reason
> To fust in us unused. Now, whether it be
> Bestial oblivion, or some craven scruple
> Of thinking too precisely on the event,—
> A thought which, quarter'd, hath but one part
>   wisdom
> And ever three parts coward,—I do not know
> Why yet I live to say 'This thing's to do,'
> Sith I have cause, and will, and strength, and means
> To do't.

Hamlet is here of course referring to the specific action of revenge, and commentators have been quick to point out that in regard to outward action he is neither slow nor a coward. But there is another and more important sense in which his self-accusation here is entirely justified, in which he is indeed 'lapsed in time and passion'—that is, as Dover Wilson explains, arrested or taken prisoner ('lapsed') by circumstances and passion. Hamlet, as everyone says, is an intellectual, but he does little enough effective thinking on the moral and metaphysical problems that beset him: his god-like reason is clogged and impeded by the emotions of disgust, revulsion and self-contempt that bring him back, again and again, to the isolation of his obsession. Effective thinking, in the regions that most concern Hamlet, implies a capacity for self-forgetfulness and a capacity for true relationship.

With this, I think, we reach the heart of the play. If, as I said earlier in these lectures, in the world of the play there is, on the one hand death, on the other, life lived with a peculiarly crude vigour of self-assertion, in such a world where are values to be found? If we are true to our direct impressions we must admit that *that* is Hamlet's problem, and questions concerning the authenticity of the Ghost or the means whereby Claudius may be trapped are subordinate to it. Hamlet's question, the question that he is continually asking himself, is, How can I live? What shall I do to rid myself of this numbing sense of meaninglessness brought by the knowledge of corruption? But behind this, and implicit in the play as a whole, is the question of being, of the activated consciousness. Hamlet comes close to putting this question directly in the great central soliloquy, but he glides away from it. And no wonder, for the problem is insoluble in the state of unresolved emotion in which he delivers himself of his thoughts; as Coleridge was never tired of insisting, thinking at the higher levels is an activity of the personality as a whole.

Perhaps, before attempting our final analysis, this is a matter that we may pause to consider, for it is of great importance; and I should like to quote from an admirable paper by Professor Dorothy Emmet called *Coleridge on the Growth of the Mind*:[1]

> Yet a further condition of the creative growth of the mind is moral integrity . . . Our thinking is bound up with our characters as morally responsible people. Yet Coleridge can distinguish between the kind of conscientiousness which can stultify the growth of the mind and the kind which is its condition. A strong sense of duty may be 'the effect of selfness in a mind incapable of gross self-interest. I mean the decrease of hope and joy, the soul in its round and round flight forming narrower circles, till at every gyre its wings beat against the *personal self*.' *The decrease of hope and joy*: in writing of Pitt, Coleridge remarked that 'his sincerity had no living root of affection'; and again, that 'the searcher after truth must love and be beloved'. For the creative power of the mind depends in the last resort on a deep underlying state which Coleridge calls Joy. Here the *locus classicus* is the *Dejection Ode*.

As Professor Emmet indicates, Coleridge's central concern is with the interrelation of all our faculties, with the need, as he puts it elsewhere, 'to keep alive the heart in the head', for 'deep thinking is attainable only by a man of deep feeling, and . . . all truth is a species of revelation'. Among the objects that he ascribes to

---

[1] *Bulletin of the John Rylands Library*, Vol. 34, No. 2, March, 1952.

himself in *The Friend* is 'to make the reason spread light over our feelings, to make our feelings, with their vital warmth, actualize our reason'; for, as he goes on to remark, '. . . in the moral being lies the source of the intellectual. The first step to knowledge, or rather the first condition of all insight into truth, is to dare commune with our very and permanent self'.[1] What all these quotations indicate is that in matters of essential concern, 'knowledge' is not simply deduction from experiment or the end of a logical process, it is a function of being, for *Quantum sumus scimus*, as we are, so we know.

[1] *Biographia Literaria* (ed. Shawcross), Vol. I, p. 98; letter to Poole, March 23, 1801; *The Friend*, General Introduction, Essays XV and XVI.

IV

I

THERE is, perhaps, no well-known passage in Shakespeare that has been found so perplexing as that in which Hamlet communes with himself between the preparation of the play to catch the conscience of the king and its performance—'To be, or not to be, that is the question . . .' It can perplex for various reasons, one of them being the variety of different explanations of crucial phrases that can reasonably be made. (In the Furness Variorum edition the text completely disappears for a couple of pages whilst a footnote marshals conflicting interpretations of the opening and general tenor; at a rough estimate the 34 lines of the soliloquy have some 440 lines of small-type commentary.) Another reason is that the speech is almost too well-known for its features to be seen distinctly, as Charles Lamb said:

> I confess myself utterly unable to appreciate that celebrated soliloquy in *Hamlet*, beginning, 'To be, or not to be,' or to tell whether it be good, bad, or indifferent; it has been so handled and pawed about by declamatory boys and men, and torn so inhumanly from its living place and principle of continuity in the play, till it has become to me a perfectly dead member.[1]

Perhaps we need not be too much dismayed; the

---

[1] Quoted in the Furness Variorum edition.

meaning may be simpler—even if in some ways subtler—than is commonly supposed. Since the speech is crucial I must ask your indulgence whilst I read it, indicating as best I may the stopping of the good Quarto, which is considerably lighter than that in most current editions.[1]

> To be, or not to be, that is the question,
> Whether 'tis nobler in the mind to suffer
> The slings and arrows of outrageous fortune,
> Or to take arms against a sea of troubles,
> And by opposing, end them, to die to sleep
> No more, and by a sleep, to say we end
> The heart-ache, and the thousand natural shocks
> That flesh is heir to; 'tis a consummation
> Devoutly to be wished to die to sleep,
> To sleep, perchance to dream, ay there's the rub,
> For in that sleep of death what dreams may come
> When we have shuffled off this mortal coil
> Must give us pause, there's the respect
> That makes calamity of so long life:
> For who would bear the whips and scorns of time,
> Th' oppressor's wrong, the proud man's contumely,
> The pangs of disprized love, the law's delay,
> The insolence of office, and the spurns
> That patient merit of th' unworthy takes,
> When he himself might his quietus make
> With a bare bodkin; who would fardels bear,
> To grunt and sweat under a weary life,
> But that the dread of something after death,

[1] It is hardly necessary for me to say that I am indebted to Professor Dover Wilson for calling attention to the punctuation of the good Quarto. See *The Manuscript of Shakespeare's 'Hamlet'* pp. 192-215, especially, in the present connexion, p. 210. In the New Cambridge edition of the play Professor Wilson modifies the Quarto punctuation slightly, whilst keeping the general fluid movement of the lines.

The undiscovered country, from whose bourn
No traveller returns, puzzles the will,
And makes us rather bear those ills we have,
Than fly to others that we know not of.
Thus conscience does make cowards of us all,
And thus the native hue of resolution
Is sicklied o'er with the pale cast of thought,
And enterprises of great pitch and moment,
With this regard their currents turn awry,
And lose the name of action. . . .

There is no need for me to do more than remind you
of the main puzzles. Does 'To be, or not to be' refer to
a contemplated action, to the continuation of Hamlet's
life, or to survival after death? When he speaks of 'The
undiscover'd country from whose bourn No traveller
returns', has he forgotten the Ghost, or has he given up
belief in its honesty? What is the meaning of that
'conscience' that makes cowards of us all, or indeed of
'thought'? And so on. It is of course clear that among
the thoughts in Hamlet's mind are thoughts of action
against the King, of suicide, and of the nature of life
after death, but the transitions are not clear, and as
soon as we attempt to give an exact paraphrase we
run into difficulties. At this point we may resort to
Dr Johnson, whose note on the passage begins:

> Of this celebrated soliloquy, which bursting from
> a man distracted with contrariety of desires, and
> overwhelmed with the magnitude of his own pur-
> poses, is connected rather in the speaker's mind, than
> on his tongue, I shall endeavour to discover the
> train, and to shew how one sentiment produces
> another.

This he proceeds to do, and I must say with considerable success, so far as success is possible; but the essential point is in his opening comment: it is the speech of a man 'distracted with contrariety of desires', and the connexions are 'rather in the speaker's mind, than on his tongue'. In other words it is not paraphrasable, and the reasons why it is not so are of some interest.

It is of course true that poetry that without loss of meaning could be put into other words would cease to be poetry. But we all know that there is a great deal of poetry of which we can usefully make for ourselves a tentative prose translation as a way of getting to grips with the full poetic meaning. Now there are passages in Shakespeare (as indeed in other poets) where even this tentative and exploratory procedure is of a very limited usefulness indeed, for what we are given is not the poetic apprehension of thought, but thought in the process of formation. Such a passage is the speech of Macbeth in the moment of temptation ('This supernatural soliciting Cannot be ill; cannot be good . . .') where we are directly aware both of the emotional and the bodily accompaniments of a state of being issuing in a conception that will not easily yield itself to conceptual forms ('my though, whose murder yet is but fantastical . . .'). Such again is that other great soliloquy, 'If it were done, when 'tis done . . .' where the meaning is composed of an emotional current running full tilt against an attempted logical control. In the *Hamlet* passage the pace is more meditative, but such ideas as it contains are held loosely in relation to a current of feeling which is the main determinant of meaning. And this is important, because the thought that is struggling for expression is one that can only be clarified on certain conditions: the necessary condition, as we saw at the end of the last lecture, is an emotional integrity and a wholeness of the personality that Hamlet has not, so far, achieved, from which indeed, as soon as the soliloquy is ended, he decisively withdraws.

The thought struggling for expression to which I just now referred is contained in the arresting opening line, 'To be, or not to be, that is the question . . .' Dr Johnson expressed his sense of the opening in these words:

> *Hamlet*, knowing himself injured in the most enormous and atrocious degree, and seeing no means of redress, but such as must expose him to the extremity of hazard, meditates on his situation in this manner: *Before I can form any rational scheme of action under this pressure of distress*, it is necessary to decide, whether, *after our present state, we are* to be or not to be. That is the question, which, as it shall be answered, will determine, *whether 'tis nobler*, and more suitable to the dignity of reason, *to suffer the outrages of fortune* patiently, or to take arms against *them*, and by opposing end them, *though perhaps* with the loss of life.

Now I feel sure that Johnson is right in implicitly rejecting the idea of suicide at this point, and I think that the idea of immortality is indeed very close to the forefront of Hamlet's consciousness. But there is that in Johnson's phrasing which partially obscures the full implications of the crucial phrase. The primary thought is not whether 'after our present state' we are to be or not to be; it is the questions of present being.[1]

In the Fourth Book of Boethius's *Consolation of Philosophy*[2] there is a notable passage that throws some light on this. Wicked men, says Boethius, are fundamentally 'destitute of all forces'.

> For why do they follow vices, forsaking virtues? By ignorance of that which is good? But what is more devoid of strength than blind ignorance? Or do they know what they should embrace, but passion driveth them headlong the contrary way? So also intemperance makes them frail, since they cannot strive against vice. Or do they wittingly and willingly forsake goodness, and decline to vices? But in this sort they leave not only to be powerful, but even to be at all (*sed omnino esse desinunt*). For they which leave the common end of all things which are, leave also being. Which may perhaps seem strange to some, that we should say that evil men are not at all, who are the greatest part of men: but yet it is so. For I deny not that evil men are evil, but withal I say that purely and simply they are not.
>
> For as thou mayest call a carcase a dead man, but not simply a man, so I confess that the vicious are evil, but I cannot grant that they are absolutely. For that is which retaineth order, and keepeth nature, but that which faileth from this leaveth also to be that which is in his own nature.

I feel the more justified in invoking this passage for the light it may throw in so far as it is clear from *Macbeth*

---

[1] I am conscious of a debt here to Max Plowman. See 'Some Values in *Hamlet*', *The Right to Live*, pp. 156 ff.

[2] Book IV, Prose ii, which is said to be a paraphrase of Plato's *Gorgias*.

that Shakespeare was deeply familiar with the traditional doctrine of the nothingness of evil—*malum nihil
est*, evil is nothing, as Boethius says a few lines after the
ending of the passage I have just given. Not indeed that
evil deeds and evil passions do not exist; it is simply
that they lead away from what all men naturally desire,
and for which goodness and being are alternative
names.[1] Neither do I offer the passage as anything like
a direct source. I quote it simply as an indication of the
kind of ideas with which Shakespeare and his educated
contemporaries were likely to be familiar, and therefore of the implications of language that would be
present to them, but that we are likely to miss: in the
passage that I have quoted, in the translation of I.T.
of 1609, the words 'to be', 'are' and 'is' are used abso-
lutely to indicate essential being. The guiding theme of
the *Consolation* is that to be free of the shackles of passion
and ignorance is to rise superior to Fortune, so that
suffering itself becomes a positive act.[2] It is for this very
reasons we may notice, that Hamlet admires Horatio.

> Since my dear soul was mistress of her choice,
> And could of men distinguish, her election
> Hath seal'd thee for herself; for thou hast been
> As one, in suffering all, that suffers nothing;
> A man that Fortune's buffets and rewards
> Hath ta'en with equal thanks; and bless'd are those
> Whose blood and judgment are so well commingled

[1] On the relation of Shakespeare's thought to traditional doctrine
in this respect see W. C. Curry, *Shakespeare's Philosophical Patterns*
(Louisiana State University Press).

[2] For the relation of Boethius's fortitude and Christian attitudes to
suffering, see John F. Danby, *Poets on Fortune's Hill*, pp. 80-83. In
Chapter IV, '*King Lear* and Christian Patience', Professor Danby writes
well of the positive implications of Christian patience.

That they are not a pipe for Fortune's finger
To sound what stop she please. Give me that man
That is not passion's slave, and I will wear him
In my heart's core, ay, in my heart of hearts,
As I do thee.

Hamlet's deep underlying concern is with essential being.

What it seems to me that Hamlet is saying at the opening of the soliloquy is that what it means to be is the question of all questions; 'and this is so,' he goes on, 'whether we believe with Boethius that the blows of Fortune must be endured, or whether we think it better actively to combat evil—which, in my case, is likely to result in my own death'—

Or to take arms against a sea of troubles,
And by opposing, end them, to die to sleep
No more . . .

But by now there is no pretence of following a logical sequence of thought; one idea blends with another—killing Claudius, killing oneself, the well-nigh insupportable troubles of life, the fear of futurity—all carried by currents of half-expressed emotion, so that the thoughts that the Prince is trying to bring into some order are eroded and carried away on the stream of feeling. Now the strongest feeling, which takes charge with the equation of death and sleep, is, as we have seen, the regressive desire to evade, shuffle off, the complexities of consciousness. Of that I do not think there can be any doubt at all—

'tis a consummation
Devoutly to be wished to die to sleep . . .

But if life is a load, death, or what may come after death, is even more to be feared. As Mr John Vyvyan has remarked in his recent book, *The Shakespearean Ethic*, 'Throughout the long soliloquy, every idea is negative. To live is to "bear the whips and scorns of time", to die is to fly to other ills "we know not of". Even the possibility of joy is excluded'; and 'when life loses joy, it also loses meaning'. For Hamlet, therefore, in his present state of conflicting feelings and restricted consciousness, no solution is possible, neither of his great problem, 'to be, or not to be', nor of the problems that entirely depend on an answer to that overriding question—the problems, I mean, of how to face life and death with something quite other than fear and aversion. What he reproaches himself with is excess of conscience—'Thus conscience does make cowards of us all'—whereas it is quite clear that, whether we take the word in the sense of reflection and consciousness or in the more usual sense of moral concern (and I agree with D. G. James that here both meanings are present), what Hamlet needs is not less of conscience but more.[1]

Thus conscience does make cowards of us all,
And thus the native hue of resolution
Is sicklied o'er with the pale cast of thought,
And enterprises of great pitch and moment,
With this regard their currents turn awry,
And lose the name of action. . . .

[1] Perhaps, in passing, we may recall that in *Richard III* it was one of the murderers of the Duke of Clarence who declared of conscience, 'it makes a man a coward . . . 'Tis a blushing shamefast spirit, that mutinies in a man's bosom; it fills a man full of obstacles: . . . it is turn'd out of towns and cities for a dangerous thing; and every man that means to live well endeavours to trust to himself and to live without it'.

It does not matter that in Hamlet's mind the thought of suicide merges with the thought of killing the king; what matters is the quite unambiguous sense of health giving way to disease, of a loss of purpose and a lapsing from positive direction. What the soliloquy does in short is to bring to a head our recognition of the dependence of thought on deeper levels of consciousness, and to make plain beyond all doubt that the set of Hamlet's consciousness is towards a region where no resolution is possible at all.

II

The soliloquy of course occupies a central point in the action. It is followed at once by the scene with Ophelia on which we have already had occasion to comment, and which makes fully explicit the direction of the emotional current of the soliloquy. To quote John Vyvyan again, the dialogue with Ophelia 'is really a continuation of the death theme; indeed, it is more, it is part of the long-drawn act of spiritual suicide'. What Ophelia says when Hamlet has left her is:

Oh, what a noble mind is here o'erthrown!
The courtier's, soldier's, scholar's, eye, tongue, sword;
The expectancy and rose of the fair state,
The glass of fashion and the mould of form,
The observed of all observers, quite, quite down!
And I, of ladies most deject and wretched,
That suck'd the honey of his music vows,
Now see that noble and most sovereign reason,
Like sweet bells jangled out of tune, and harsh;
That unmatch'd form and feature of blown youth
Blasted with ecstasy; Oh, woe is me,
To have seen what I have seen, see what I see!

That surely is quite explicit, and from now until the closing scene it seems to me that little detailed commentary is needed to enforce the view that I have been trying to define. Hamlet, with whatever excitements of his reason and his blood, is a man who has given himself over to a false direction of consciousness; and at each of the crucial points of the action Shakespeare leaves us in no doubt of the inadequacy—and worse—of Hamlet's basic attitudes. The play scene, which includes the obscene jesting with Ophelia, ends with the declaration,

'Tis now the very witching time of night,
When churchyards yawn, and hell itself breathes out
Contagion to this world; now could I drink hot
    blood,
And do such bitter business as the day
Would quake to look on . . .

—and indeed there is contagion from hell in the words addressed to the ostensibly praying Claudius. The scene with his mother includes the killing of Polonius and Hamlet's almost perfunctory repentance; whilst the attempt to break Gertrude's attachment to Claudius, to show her the truth of her false position, is subtly changed in character by Hamlet's obsessive preoccupation with what he denounces. Once more, before Hamlet disappears from the action for a time, he is allowed to reveal himself in a soliloquy which contains a firm though implicit placing judgment. It is, you remember, when Hamlet, about to embark for England, is informed of the expedition of Fortinbras—the same Fortinbras who, earlier in the play, had

'shark'd up a list of lawless resolutes' to regain the land
lost by his father to the elder Hamlet. Dissuaded from
that enterprise he is now leading his army against
Poland,

> to gain a little patch of ground
> That hath in it no profit but the name.

It is by this expedition that Hamlet feels himself
admonished—

> How all occasions do inform against me,
> And spur my dull revenge!

As before, our interest is evenly divided between what
is said and what is implied. What Hamlet says is that
these clear signs of making for a defined objective
reproach his own inactivity:

> Sure he that made us with such large discourse,
> Looking before and after, gave us not
> That capability and god-like reason
> To fust in us unused . . .

—nor, we may add, to use for purposes such as those
of the Fortinbrases of this world. And that surely is the
dramatic point of the scene. As in the earlier soliloquy
after the encounter with the Players, Hamlet is indulging himself with thoughts of a way out of his impasse
that is no way out, and the terms in which he expresses
his sense of inferiority indicate how far that ranging
mind has allowed itself to be restricted.

> Examples, gross as earth, exhort me;
> Witness this army of such mass and charge,

Led by a delicate and tender prince,
Whose spirit with divine ambition puff'd
Makes mouths at the invisible event;
Exposing what is mortal and unsure
To all that fortune, death and danger dare,
Even for an egg-shell. Rightly to be great
Is not to stir without great argument,
But greatly to find quarrel in a straw
When honour's at the stake.

Professor Dover Wilson paraphrases the last sentence:
'Fighting for trifles is mere pugnacity, not greatness;
but it *is* greatness to fight instantly and for a trifle when
honour is at stake'. Right enough; but this is arguing
in a circle, for it leaves honour as no more than the
prompting to fight instantly and for a trifle—

a plot
Whereon the numbers cannot try the cause,
Which is not tomb enough and continent
To hide the slain.

'Honour' here is not a defining word but a mere
justifying blur. Since the author of *Henry IV*, Part I,
was not likely to be uncritical of such 'honour', nor
to believe that the ambition prompting Fortinbras was
indeed divine, the purpose of the soliloquy can only be
to define one further stage in the withdrawal of
Hamlet's consciousness, a sacrifice of reason to a
fantasy of quite unreflective destructive action; and
indeed the soliloquy ends with explicit emphasis—

O, from this time forth,
My thoughts be bloody, or be nothing worth!

For three scenes Hamlet is absent from the action.[1] When he returns, he is shown first as brooding on death with an exclusive intensity, then as reacting to the poignant reminder of the love that he denied with a long outburst in which there is neither self-knowledge nor sincerity—

> Nay, as thou'lt mouth,
> I'll rant as well as thou.

Neither does the opening of the next scene, the final one of the play, do anything to restore our memory of the man whose own highest standards were made explicit in the noble eulogy of human potentiality—

> What a piece of work is a man, how noble in reason, how infinite in faculties, in form and moving, how like an angel in apprehension, how like a god!

Now, what we have instead is a demonstration of quickness of mind used in a triumph that is either barbaric or trivial. Rosencrantz and Guildenstern have been sent to their deaths 'not shriving time allowed', and 'they are not near my conscience'. As for the encounter with Osric, this serves both to demonstrate one more facet of King Claudius's world and at the same time to underline the only kind of relief that Hamlet now finds possible—a satirical display of the world's folly.

[1] Though he is kept in our minds not only by the frequent references to him and by his letters to Horatio and the King, but by Ophelia and Laertes: by Ophelia because her madness and death are the result of Hamlet's own actions, by Laertes because, as Mr John Vyvyan says, he represents the uninhibited vengeance to which Hamlet has now given himself up. On this, and the 'allegorical' overtones of these two figures see *The Shakespearean Ethic*, pp. 50 ff.

III

And now a strange thing happens, so strange that even those who by no means share the romantic idealization of Hamlet, feel justified in claiming that at the end his nobility is restored. This Hamlet, who has shown himself so torn and distracted, suddenly appears composed, with a fortitude that has in it nothing of the emotional heightening—of at times the near hysteria—that has accompanied his courage on former occasions. Osric has done his errand, the royal party is approaching, and there is a pause before the last desperate action.

> *Horatio.* You will lose this wager, my lord.
> *Hamlet.* I do not think so. Since he went into France, I have been in continual practice. I shall win at the odds; but thou wouldst not think how ill all's here about my heart—but it is no matter.
> *Horatio.* Nay, good my lord—
> *Hamlet.* It is but foolery, but it is such a kind of gain-giving as would perhaps trouble a woman.
> *Horatio.* If your mind dislike anything, obey it. I will forestall their repair hither, and say you are not fit.
> *Hamlet.* Not a whit, we defy augury. There is a special providence in the fall of a sparrow. If it be now, 'tis not to come—if it be not to come, it will be now—if it be not now, yet it will come—the readiness is all. Since no man, of aught he leaves, knows what is't to leave betimes, let be.

In my second lecture I made a truncated quotation from Professor C. S. Lewis which I must now give in its entirety. 'The world of *Hamlet* is a world where one has lost one's way. The Prince also has no doubt lost his, and we can tell the precise moment at which he finds it again'—it is the moment when he defies augury in those quiet, memorable but puzzling words that I have just quoted from the play. The Prince has lost his way, 'and we can tell the precise moment at which he finds it again'. Others have written to the same effect. But is it really so? If we take the view that this is a tragic hero who has indeed lost his way and who will shortly lose his life, but who has in some fundamental way come through, are we not in danger of losing sight of a fundamental principle of Shakespearean construction—of a fundamental principle indeed of all supreme works of art—that no passage has its full meaning in isolation from the whole of which it forms a part? Perhaps, for the last time, we may remind ourselves of other of Shakespeare's plays, so that comparison may help us to determine how we should take the matter before us.

In all the scenes in which Shakespeare's tragic characters confront their deaths there is a mystery that partially confounds our rational analysis and explanation. There is a profound remark of Blake's to the effect that we should distinguish between states and individuals in those states. Now whether we regard Shakespeare's characters as individuals or as dramatic embodiments of states of being, Shakespeare's generosity, his outgoing feeling for life in all its forms, even when life is perverted and self-defeated, plays about them at their end. All that can be said on their behalf *is* said, either directly or in the less explicit statement of the full dramatic action. There is, for example,

Brutus, whose funeral eulogy is so far from being merely formal:

> This was the noblest Roman of them all.
> All the conspirators save only he
> Did that they did in envy of great Caesar;
> He only, in a general honest thought
> And common good to all, made one of them.
> His life was gentle, and the elements
> So mix't in him, that Nature might stand up
> And say to all the world, 'This was a man!'

Or there is Coriolanus, whose foreknowledge of death gives dignity to his yielding to the instinct he had professed to despise:

> O mother, mother!
> What have you done? Behold, the heavens do ope,
> The gods look down, and this unnatural scene
> They laugh at. O my mother, mother! O!
> You have won a happy victory to Rome;
> But for your son, believe it, O, believe it,
> Most dangerously you have with him prevail'd,
> If not most mortal to him. But let it come.

Here indeed, in each instance, is nobility and genuine pathos. Yet neither of these passages stands in isolation: each of them comes at the culminating point of a dramatic structure of which the full force is now present to us—that is, unless we are prepared to sacrifice Shakespeare's complex meanings for the sake of some easy 'dramatic' effect. The word 'irony' tends to suggest some aloofness from life, a sort of pleasure in seeing through experiences that others find simply touching. Shakespeare's irony of course is not of this kind; it is simply part of his supreme intelligence; charity is not the less charity for being undeceived. In this sense, then, there is irony—a deeply tragic irony— in each of the scenes to which I just now referred. The abstract generality of Brutus's honest thoughts, the preoccupation with a political 'common good' at the expense of humanity—that is what the play taken as a whole has put in question. As for Coriolanus, neither the dignity of his mother's pleadings nor the fortitude and magnanimity of his decision can obscure what the play makes clear—that the patrician 'honour' in which Volumnia had reared him is an aggressive boy's pitiful and inadequate substitute for that integrity which is at once an individual and a civic virtue.

To all this—for examples could be multiplied— Hamlet's death is no exception. By what he says, by what others say about him ('noble Hamlet', 'noble heart', 'sweet Prince'), is recalled that other Hamlet whom Ophelia knew—'The expectancy and rose of the fair state'—but who has appeared so fitfully in the course of the present action, the 'sweet bells' of his reason being 'jangled out of tune, and harsh'. 'The readiness is all', he says, meaning, I take it, not simply preparedness for death but that quality for which Sir Thomas Elyot, declaring that English lacked a name for it, had taken from Latin the word 'maturity'.

'Maturum' in Latin may be interpreted ripe or ready, as fruit when it is ripe, it is at the very point to be gathered and eaten. And every other thing, when it is ready, it is at the instant after to be occupied. Therefore that word maturity, is translated to the acts of man, that when they be done with such moderation, that nothing in the doing may be seen superfluous or indigent, we may say, that they be maturely done.[1]

Hamlet's 'readiness', then, is that maturity of the feeling, thinking being that enables a man to be 'as one, in suffering all, that suffers nothing'. The thought—as well as Elyot's phrasing—will be echoed in *King Lear*:

> men must endure
> Their going hence, even as their coming hither;
> Ripeness is all.

But whereas in *Lear* Edgar's sentence carries a large part of the burden of the play, indicating as it does that responsiveness to life in which 'the "I" in the individual' ceases to be in the centre of the picture and personal action takes on an almost impersonal quality, Hamlet's utterance can in no sense be regarded as indicating the goal towards which his consciousness, the central consciousness of the play, has been directed. What it represents rather is the paradoxical recognition of a truth glimpsed in defeat, and by this I mean defeat in terms of Hamlet's own highest standards. All that Hamlet is now ready for is to meet his death in playing the part of the avenger, the part imposed on him by that Ghost whose command had been for a sterile concentration on death and evil. Art, says Pasternak's Zhivago, 'has two constant, two unending preoccupa-

[1] Sir Thomas Elyot, *The Governour* (1531), Book I, Chapter xxii. Elyot is here beginning his exposition of the ways in which dancing may be an introduction to the cardinal virtue of Prudence, and the branch here indicated is the mean between celerity and slowness. The whole chapter has, I think, some bearing on Shakespeare's play.

tions: it is always meditating upon death and it is always thereby creating new life'. To recognize the truth in this it is necessary to supply an unspoken condition: that the meditation on death is no mere brooding but an energetic and transforming assimilation of the basic facts of the human condition. What Hamlet represents, on the other hand, is a fixation of consciousness—a condition in which neither death nor life can be truly known.

I said at the beginning that this account of *Hamlet* would be in some ways tentative, and I hope that no one will take my exposition as more than a challenge to re-read and re-think the play. What I have tried to do is to suggest that we are likely to see *Hamlet* more clearly if we see it as one of a series of studies of the mind's engagement with the world, of the intimate and intricate relations of self and world. In each of these plays—I have named *Othello*, *Timon*, and some others—there is an exploration of the ways in which 'being' and 'knowing' are related, so that failure in being, the corruption of consciousness, results either in a false affirmation, as with Othello, or in an inability to affirm at all, as with Hamlet. In *King Lear*, where so many lines of Shakespeare's thought converge, Lear only comes to 'see better' through a purgatorial progress of self-knowledge which enables him finally to respond to love. Perhaps we may say that Hamlet's consciousness is not unlike the consciousness of the unregenerate Lear, full of the knowledge of bitter wrong, of evil seemingly inherent in human nature. But Hamlet, unlike Lear—even if, initially, he is less greatly sinning —cannot break out of the closed circle of loathing and self-contempt, so that his nature is 'subdued to what it works in, like the dyer's hand'. The awareness that he embodies is at best an intermediate stage of the spirit, at worst a blind alley. Most certainly Hamlet's way of knowing the world is not Shakespeare's own.

Printed in Great Britain
at Hopetoun Street, Edinburgh,
by T. and A. CONSTABLE LTD.
Printers to the University of Edinburgh

These are lectures — what effect must? time constraints have upon them?

And the audience gets lots of refs to other critics + their work.

Hamlet may be a man who cannot make up his mind, but the play is about death.
(2nd lecture)

Does not go outside the play, except, occasionally, to the playwright and except to clarify a point by contrast with another's work.